AGELESS BY DESIGN

My 13 Laws for Intentional Living

Michael Rouleau

FOREVER 59 PRESS

Ageless by Design: My 13 Laws for Intentional Living

Copyright © 2026 by Michael Rouleau

All rights reserved.

This book is for informational and educational purposes only. It reflects the author's personal experience, research, and opinions. It is not intended to provide medical advice, diagnose health conditions, or replace the guidance of a qualified healthcare professional. Always consult your physician or other licensed provider before making changes to your exercise, nutrition, medication, or health-related routines. The author and publisher disclaim any liability arising from the use or application of the information contained in this book.

ISBN: 979-8-9956889-0-7

Library of Congress Control Number: 2026909539

Published by FOREVER 59 PRESS

Cary, North Carolina

Cover design by Ann Rouleau.

Interior design by Michael Rouleau.

Printed in the United States of America.

10 9 8 7 6 5 4 3 2 1

For Ann — my Forever 59 life partner

Table of Contents

INTRODUCTION

Most books about aging start with a promise. This one starts with a moment I'll never forget.

When my father retired in his 60s, his world quietly collapsed inward. Work had been his only social outlet, and once it was gone, the connections that held his life together slowly unraveled. He lived alone, a hundred miles from the nearest family. His friends were still working. His days became smaller. His meals came from the freezer. His exercise was limited to rolling trash cans back from the curb — his and the neighbors'.

By the time my family visited him for Easter, something felt wrong. I checked him into his local hospital, hoping it was something simple. It wasn't. His kidneys were failing. Every day I met with the nephrologist, hoping for a plan, a sign of improvement, anything. But the decline continued. On Mother's Day, at age 75, he took his last breath, and I was there with him.

Losing him that way changed me. It forced me to confront aging not as an abstract concept, but as a lived reality — one that can unfold slowly or all at once, depending on the choices we make and the support we have. I realized I needed to do better. Not out of fear, but out of responsibility. I wanted to be present for my family. I wanted to live with joy, not drift toward decline. I wanted to age with intention.

That moment became the spark for everything in this book.

I didn't set out to chase longevity for its own sake. I set out to build a life that stays wide, connected, strong, and meaningful for as long as I'm lucky enough to live it. And I learned something along the way: confidence comes from competence — in your habits, your health, your mindset, your systems. Aging well isn't a mystery. It's a practice.

This book isn't about perfection. Perfection is a prison. It's about intentionality. Experimentation. Consistency. Joy. And the belief that aging slowly is less about adding years and more about adding life to the years you already have.

You won't find theories here. You'll find what I actually do — the routines, the metrics, the experiments, the mistakes, the course corrections, the mindset shifts, and the systems that keep me moving forward. Each chapter begins with a principle, a "Law of Aging Well," but it always comes back to real life: how I live it, why it matters, and what it has taught me.

If you're looking for a magic pill, you won't find it here. If you're looking for a blueprint you can actually follow — one built from lived experience, real data, and a deep desire to stay fully alive — you're in the right place.

Now that I'm 62 years young (forever 59 to those who ask), I can look back over the decade and a half since losing my father with a real sense of pride. I've rebuilt my life through the same principles I share in this book. I've ridden more than 10,000 miles on the bike in a single year, dropped the 35 pounds that held me back for years, and brought my body fat percentage down to a level that makes most guys half my age take notice. I returned to graduate school to study psychology and mental skills to better understand how people change and why they don't. I've built systems that let me train consistently, learn continuously, nurture relationships, and live with more energy, joy, and purpose than I had in my thirties. None of this came from hacks or shortcuts. It came from daily, intentional choices — the same choices these laws are built on. It wasn't perfect. I made mistakes. I course corrected. I learned as I went. If your life could benefit from this kind of change, I invite you to read on.

Let's get to work. Your future self is waiting.

PART I — LAYING THE FOUNDATION

Part I is about getting ready — not with gear or checklists, but with the mindset and inner clarity that make everything else possible. Aging well starts long before the habits and routines; it begins with the beliefs and intentions that shape how you move through the world. These first two laws — Purpose and Competence — form that inner framework. Purpose points you toward what matters. Competence reminds you that you can meet the challenges ahead. Together, they shift you from reacting to leading your own life.

CHAPTER 1 — THE LAW OF PURPOSE

The law of purpose is simple: You stop drifting the moment you decide to steer.

Graduating from high school in 1981 felt like stepping into a world where the path ahead was simple and predictable. I was on the "college track," and the formula seemed obvious: go to a good school, get a degree, land a solid job, marry, raise a family. That was the plan — or at least the assumption.

College admissions back then were almost quaint. My application to North Carolina State University fit on something not much bigger than a postcard. No essays. No curated list of humanitarian achievements. Unlike today's youth aiming for higher education, I felt no pressure to have saved the world before turning eighteen. If you had the grades, the coursework, and the SAT scores, you were in.

One afternoon at the end of my junior year at NCSU, I was checking my posted exam scores when my professor opened his office door and asked if I was free for the summer. He was doing some consulting for a major telecommunications company and needed a college kid to help. The job paid an incredible $9 an hour — more than double what I was making as a maintenance helper at a printing company. That moment, that tiny stroke of timing and luck, became my first real career break. It led to a permanent job after graduation, a degree in Industrial Engineering completed in 3.5 years, and the start of a life that felt like it was unfolding exactly as it should.

A year later, my high school sweetheart graduated from NC State. We got married, bought a house, adopted a dog, and lived the DINK (dual income, no kids) dream. Life was good. Simple. Predictable. We were living the post-high school life we had assumed would just happen — including the cutest little cocker spaniel puppy named Alex.

Ten years into our marriage, our first child arrived — and everything changed in the best possible way. Four years after that, our second child was born. My wife initially returned to work after our first, but within a month we realized she wanted to be home full time. After our second was born, she was offered her old job back, and that opened a door for me: I became a full-time dad of a newborn and a four-year old while starting my own business incubator from home. Her income covered the bills, giving me the freedom to build something without the pressure of immediate success.

A few years later, the telecommunications company she worked for collapsed under a series of management missteps. She was one of the last employees left — the one who literally turned out the lights. By then, my business had grown enough for her to come home again and help me run it. We've worked side by side ever since, raising our kids and building a life together. Today, we're still running that small company in our 60s.

Why share all this? Because it shows something important: I didn't have a master plan. If anything, my life could be titled Serendipity. I drifted from opportunity to opportunity, reacting more than directing. I happened to be standing outside a professor's door at the right moment. My wife happened to get a call from a former coworker at exactly the right time. We worked hard, yes, but we were also lucky. As the saying goes, the harder I worked, the luckier I got.

That same pattern showed up in my health. I was active, but not intentionally. I played sports as a kid, took the required fitness classes in college, and dabbled in various activities as an adult — golf, sailing, sporting clays. But nothing was structured. Nothing was purposeful.

My diet followed the same drift. I went from 130 pounds in high school to over 180 by the time I got married. I held that weight into my 40s until a physical revealed sky-high cholesterol. Off to the dietician I went.

Life felt good. We were young, our business was thriving, our kids were growing, and I wasn't thinking much about the future. The future was something that was way out beyond the horizon.

Then Mother's Day 2010 arrived.

I was 46 years old, sitting beside my father as he took his last breath. He was only 75. That didn't seem old anymore. His decline had been rapid and brutal — a collapse that began years earlier when he retired, lost his social structure, and slowly withdrew from the world. Watching him fade forced me to confront something I had avoided: my own mortality.

Life got real, fast.

In the weeks that followed, I sat down with a piece of paper and started writing. I looked at where I'd come from, what brought me joy, what responsibilities I carried, and where all those threads intersected. I examined my strengths, my shortcomings, my habits, and my drift. I realized I wanted to take better care of myself so I could take care of the people I loved. I wanted to push myself, to grow, and to stop drifting.

So I started reading. And reading. And reading. Psychology grabbed me — especially the science of optimal performance. Eventually, the reading wasn't enough. At 54, I went back to school for a Master's degree in psychology with a focus on sport psychology. I still remember the admissions counselor asking if I knew I'd have to take statistics. I did. I was ready. At 55, I earned the degree.

I started a blog to share mental skills training with amateur athletes — a continuation of something I'd always been drawn to: helping others improve. That instinct had been there since the early days of my business incubator. Now it had a new direction.

From that point forward, I committed to living with purpose — in my relationships, my work, my health, and my aging. I didn't want to drift anymore. I wanted to steer.

We all have an expiration date. We don't control when it comes, but we absolutely control the condition we're in when we arrive there. That realization changed everything for me.

It was time to step up — not by one notch, but by several. Time to grab life by the horns. Time to enjoy it fully. Time to age intentionally.

The rest of this book is the story of how I've done that — and how you can, too. Every morning, I wake up with a purpose. You can, too.

Chapter Summary: The Law of Purpose

- My early life unfolded through serendipity rather than strategy. I drifted from opportunity to opportunity, reacting instead of directing.
- My health and habits followed the same pattern — active, but not intentional.
- My father's decline and death at 75 forced me to confront my own mortality.
- That moment revealed how quickly life can narrow without purpose, connection, and structure.
- I realized I needed to take better care of myself so I could take care of the people I love.
- I began examining my strengths, weaknesses, responsibilities, and desires.
- Returning to school at 54 and starting a blog were turning points in reclaiming direction.

- Purpose became the foundation for how I live, work, and age today.
- I chose to stop drifting and start steering — and that decision changed everything.

Your Turn — The Law of Purpose

You've just read my story — the drift, the luck, the wake-up call, and the moment everything shifted. Now it's time to turn the lens toward your own life. Purpose doesn't appear all at once. It begins with awareness, honesty, and a willingness to look at where you've been and where you want to go.

Take a few minutes to reflect on the questions below. Write your answers down. Don't edit. Don't judge. Just notice.

- Where in your life have you been drifting instead of steering? Think about your work, your health, your relationships, your routines.
- What responsibilities, people, or values matter most to you right now? Purpose often hides in the things we care about but haven't named.
- What experiences — good or painful — have shaped what you want your life to stand for? Your past is full of clues.
- What part of your life feels misaligned with the person you want to become? Misalignment is not failure. It's information.

- What is one small step you could take this week that moves you from drifting to steering? Purpose begins with a single intentional action.

The law of purpose is simple: You stop drifting the moment you decide to steer.

➤ IT'S NOT WHAT YOU KNOW, IT'S WHAT YOU DO. ➤

And naming your purpose is the first thing you do. But, don't worry if you aren't comfortable doing this just now. By the end of the book, you will have the tools to clearly define you own purpose.

Understanding my purpose was the moment everything shifted. But knowing why I wanted to change didn't automatically give me the confidence to do it. I needed something more solid than motivation — I needed competence. I needed to learn, to experiment, to fill the gaps in my understanding. That journey, the one that turned intention into confidence, is the heart of the next chapter.

CHAPTER 2 — THE LAW OF COMPETENCE

The law of competence is simple: Competence is the engine of confidence. Confidence is the fuel that keeps us moving toward an optimal life.

Purpose gave me direction, but moving toward that purpose required the ability to act with clarity and confidence. That's where competence enters the picture. Competence isn't about perfection or knowing everything — it's about understanding enough to make informed choices, adapt when things change, and trust yourself to keep moving. It's the steady foundation that turns intention into capability.

As I began taking my health more seriously, I realized just how much I didn't know. I had the desire to age well, but desire alone wasn't going to carry me. I needed to learn the fundamentals — not in an academic way, but in a practical, lived way. What actually keeps a body strong? What supports a sharp mind? What habits matter most? Where were my blind spots? The more I explored these questions, the more I understood that competence wasn't a luxury. It was the gateway to real, durable confidence.

As I started digging into these questions, I realized I needed a clearer framework for understanding confidence itself — what fosters it, what inhibits it, and why it matters so much for aging well. That search led me to a book that fundamentally shifted my perspective. Years ago, I read *Confidence: How Much You Really Need and How to Get It* by Thomas Chamorro-Premuzic, and it challenged the familiar "fake it till you make it" mindset that so many of us grew up hearing. It made me confront an uncomfortable truth: real confidence isn't something you project; it's something you build through competence.

That idea hit me hard. "Fake it till you make it" might get you through a presentation or a first date, but it won't sustain a lifetime of healthy aging. You can't fake your way into strength, mobility, metabolic health, emotional resilience, or longevity. You can't put lipstick on a pig and call it optimal aging. You need substance. You need to understand the inputs that keep your body and mind sharp. You need to see the gaps in your knowledge so you can fill them.

One of the voices that helped me internalize this was Emily Fletcher, whose guided meditations became part of my mental training. In her *Pep Talk* meditation, she says something that stuck with me: "perfection is a prison." She reminds us that life will not go according to plan. Mistakes are guaranteed. Setbacks are inevitable. The question isn't whether things will go wrong — it's whether we'll commit anyway.

That idea changed how I approached aging. I didn't need perfection. I needed commitment. I needed to give myself permission to succeed, even if the path wasn't flawless.

In another meditation, *Compare and Despair*, Emily warns against measuring our progress against the curated highlight reels of others — especially on social media. People post their best moments, not their real lives. If we compare our everyday reality to someone else's filtered triumphs, we'll always feel behind. And when we feel behind, we hesitate. We stall. We stop trying.

But aging well requires the opposite: we must acknowledge our own wins, however small. We can't build on success we refuse to recognize. When we celebrate our victories — our real victories, not fake, curated social media fodder — we create momentum for the next challenge.

This mindset aligns with something I've said for years: humans are messy. We make mistakes. We fall short. We overestimate our willpower and underestimate our blind spots. And that's okay. The Serenity Prayer captures this idea perfectly: accept what you can't change, change what you can, and learn to tell the difference. When we give ourselves permission to be human, life becomes a lot more enjoyable.

Competence is about direction, not perfection. It's about learning enough to make informed choices, doing the best you can with what you have, and adjusting as you go. That's what optimal aging really is — not flawless execution, but consistent, intentional improvement.

I saw this firsthand during my years working with Mitsubishi from 1989 to 1997. Their philosophy of kaizen — continuous, incremental improvement — wasn't just a business strategy. It was a way of thinking. A way of living. You don't overhaul everything at once. You make one small improvement. Then another. Then another. Over time, those small steps compound into something extraordinary. Making a 1% improvement every day is much easier to comprehend and execute than making a 100% improvement in one fell swoop.

That's how I approached my own journey. I wanted to learn as much as I could — not to become perfect, but to become competent, one small step at a time. To understand the inputs required to age well: nutrition, movement, sleep, stress management, mindset, relationships, purpose. To see the gaps in my knowledge so I could fill them. To build confidence not from pretending, but from knowing.

Chapter Summary: The Law of Competence

- Real confidence must be earned through competence, not pretending.
- Aging well requires understanding the inputs that keep the body and mind sharp.
- "Perfection is a prison" — mistakes and setbacks are inevitable, and that's okay. Commitment matters more than flawless execution.
- Comparing yourself to others undermines progress; acknowledge your own wins.

- Humans are messy — self-compassion is essential for long-term growth.
- Optimal doesn't mean perfect; it means doing the best you can right now.
- Kaizen — small, continuous improvements — is the path to sustainable change.
- Competence creates confidence, and confidence fuels an optimal life.

Your Turn: A Practice for Competence

Purpose: To identify the areas where competence will build confidence in your own aging journey.

Action Steps:

- List the areas of your life where you feel confident — and why. List the areas where you feel uncertain or under-skilled.
- Choose one area where increasing your knowledge would improve your confidence.
- Identify one small, kaizen-style step you can take this week to build competence.
- Acknowledge one recent win — no matter how small — and write it down.

Where would greater competence give you greater confidence in your life right now?

The law of competence is simple: Competence is the engine of confidence. Confidence is the fuel that keeps us moving toward an optimal life.

➤ IT'S NOT WHAT YOU KNOW, IT'S WHAT YOU DO. ➤

PART I SUMMARY — Laying the Foundation for an Optimal Life

Part I has been about preparation — not the kind that involves checklists or equipment, but the kind that happens inside your head and your heart. Before you can age well in any meaningful way, you need a foundation strong enough to support the work ahead. These first two laws — Purpose and Competence — are that foundation.

Purpose gives you direction.
Competence gives you confidence.
Together, they shift you from drifting to steering.

Now that you've clarified your purpose and begun building competence, you're ready for the nuts and bolts — the daily actions, habits, and systems that will shape your physical, mental, and emotional health for decades to come.

Part II is where the ideas become behaviors.
It's where the work becomes real.
It's where you begin turning intention into action.

PART II — TURNING INTENTION INTO ACTION

Part I laid the groundwork by helping you clarify why aging well matters and by showing you that confidence must be earned through competence. With that foundation in place, Part II shifts from mindset to mechanics. This is where we get practical. Here, we explore the daily behaviors, physiological levers, and evidence-based practices that shape how you feel, how you function, and how you age. These chapters translate purpose into routines, competence into skill, and intention into action — one small, sustainable step at a time.

CHAPTER 3 — THE LAW OF FUEL

The Law of Fuel is simple: What you put into your body determines what you can get out of it.

You can't exercise your way out of a bad diet.

Why is diet so important? Because while the human body is extraordinarily adaptable, it can only compensate for so long. We can pour an incredible variety of substances into it, and it will do its best to turn them into fuel. But if we're aiming for optimal aging, we need to be far more intentional about the types and amounts of fuel we choose to ingest.

I still vividly remember sitting in the dietician's office as she prepared two lists for me. The first list—foods I could not eat—was very long. The second list—foods I could eat—was very short. Why? Because I had not been intentional about what I stuffed (literally) into my body. I was overweight, and my cholesterol was out of control. I followed the new plan she gave me, even though I wasn't thrilled about it.

At the same time, I bought a copy of *The Duke Diet* by Howard Eisenson and Martin Binks. The key tenets of the Duke approach were straightforward:

- Structured calorie control: Roughly 1,100–1,300 calories per day for women and 1,400–1,600 for men to promote steady fat loss (not maintenance).
- Balanced macronutrients: About 40–50% carbohydrates, 20–25% protein, and 20–25% fat—not extreme, just balanced.
- Dual eating tracks: A standard balanced plan and a lower-carb option for people with specific metabolic needs.
- Lifestyle integration: Nutrition paired with individualized exercise plans to create a "calorie-burning lifestyle."
- Behavioral strategy: A major focus on changing how you think about food and movement so the calorie balance becomes sustainable long term.

That combination—structure, balance, and behavioral awareness—was my first real introduction to eating with intention rather than convenience or habit.

Did the diet work?

You bet it did. I dropped the weight pretty quickly—and as the weight dropped, so did my cholesterol. My doctor was happy. My wife was happy. I was happy.

But did I make the long-term lifestyle changes described in *The Duke Diet*?

Well, in a word—no.

Over time, the old habits crept back in. Fast food with the kids when time was short. Forgetting the calories-in/calories-out equation. Letting the quantity of fats take over. Before I knew it, the scale was showing 185 pounds again.

Using BMI alone—which is simply based on height and weight and definitely not the most robust tool for determining fitness for all body types—I should have been somewhere between 144 and 176 pounds, with a midpoint target of 160. If you've ever picked up a 25-pound dumbbell, you know how heavy it is. I was carrying that around every hour of every day.

I also learned that shooting for a single "number" on the scale was defeating. It was far easier to work within a range—something tighter than the full BMI spread, but flexible enough to account for normal fluctuations. I chose the midpoint of my BMI target (160 pounds) plus or minus five pounds as a good starting range.

If you're curious what your own range might be based solely on BMI, here's one commonly referenced chart (originally developed by MET Life in 1943).

Height	Male (lbs)	Female (lbs)
4'6"	63-77	63-77
4'7"	68-84	68-83
4'8"	74-90	72-88
4'9"	79-97	77-94
4'10"	85-103	81-99
4'11"	90-110	86-105
5'0"	95-117	90-110
5'1"	101-123	95-116
5'2"	106-130	99-121
5'3"	112-136	104-127
5'4"	117-143	108-132
5'5"	122-150	113-138
5'6"	128-156	117-143
5'7"	133-163	122-149
5'8"	139-169	126-154

Check the next page for those who are a little taller:

Height	Male (lbs)	Female (lbs)
5'9"	144-176	131-160
5'10"	149-183	135-165
5'11"	155-189	140-171
6'0"	160-196	144-176
6'1"	166-202	149-182
6'2"	171-209	153-187
6'3"	176-216	158-193
6'4"	182-222	162-198
6'5"	187-229	167-204
6'6"	193-235	171-209
6'7"	198-242	176-215
6'8"	203-249	180-220
6'9"	209-255	185-226
6'10"	214-262	189-231
6'11"	220-268	194-237
7'0"	225-275	198-242

And if you want to calculate your own BMI, the formula is easy:

BMI = Weight (Lb) / Height(in)^2 x 703

Once you have your result, you can compare it to the following table:

Underweight	18.5 and below
Healthy weight	18.5 – 24.9
Overweight	25.0 – 29.9
Obesity	30 and above

How to Calculate Your Personal Weight Range

Here's an example using a 5'3" female (the current average adult female height in the US):

1. Lower limit = 104 lbs

2. Upper limit = 127 lbs

3. Difference = 127 - 104 = 23

4. Half = 23 / 2 = 11.5

5. Midpoint = 104 + 11.5 = 115.5

6. Practical range = midpoint ± 5 lbs → 110.5–120.5 lbs

A range is more sustainable than chasing a single number.

Daily weigh-ins without perfection

Managing my weight meant daily weigh-ins. This is where our training from Chapter 2 comes in. We don't need perfection here—in fact, our weight will fluctuate due to many factors:

Eating later than usual

Being over- or under-hydrated

Eating foods that cause water retention

Timing of exercise

Illness

Normal biological variability

Daily weigh-ins work for me because I don't want to be the proverbial ostrich with his head in the sand—but I also don't want to panic from a random out-of-range reading. The direction and trend are what matter most.

And remember: what we ingest is only half of the equation. The other half—what we burn—comes in Chapter 4.

What my diet actually looks like

On paper, my diet might look more restrictive than it feels in real life. In practice, it's easy to follow month after month because it's built on consistency, simplicity, and foods I genuinely enjoy. It's not boring when the scale reports good news, when my doctor tells me my blood work is exemplary, or when I realize I no longer need multiple sizes of clothing in my closet.

This way of eating is designed to support my base metabolic rate of around 1,500 calories per day, plus the calories required for everyday activities and my workouts. Your needs may differ, but the principle is the same: fuel the body with intention, not impulse. Let's break it down by meal.

Breakfast: non-negotiable

Breakfast is non-negotiable for me—it's required to start fueling the day on the right foot. I generally have my first meal about two hours after waking, around 8:00 a.m., after starting my day at 6:00 a.m. That gives me time to get an hour or so of work done and to greet the sun with a 30-minute walk with my dog.

My breakfast is simple and consistent:

1.5–2 cups plain Cheerios topped with blueberries and other berries

Fairlife fat-free ultra-filtered milk

Beetroot juice (1 tsp beet powder mixed with water)

Ensure Max Protein shake (on non-gym mornings; otherwise after the workout)

Lunch: smoothie or simple sandwich

Most days, lunch is a smoothie. Some days, I'll substitute a sandwich (turkey, peanut butter and jam, or tuna) with a serving of chips and a glass of Fairlife milk.

But the smoothie is the backbone of my midday fuel.

Smoothie Recipes

Non-Workout Smoothie (Higher-Fat Version)

This is the version I drink when I'm not heading straight into a workout and want longer-lasting satiety.

Same base ingredients as the workout version below, plus:

1 tablespoon chia seeds — omega-3s, fiber, and gel-forming satiety

½ teaspoon fish oil — concentrated omega-3 fatty acids

1 handful lightly salted peanuts — healthy fats, protein, and long-lasting fullness – note the peanuts are not actually mixed into the smoothie, but eaten along with it.

This version digests more slowly and keeps me full for hours.

Macros:

Calories: ~694 Protein: ~46 g Carbs: ~86 g Fat: ~22 g

Fiber: ~17.5 g

Workout Smoothie (Low-Fat Version)

This is the version I drink when I'm heading straight into a workout. It digests quickly and provides clean, fast energy.

Ingredients and why they're included:

1 cup blueberries — antioxidants, fiber, natural sweetness, low glycemic load

¼ cup raspberries — additional fiber and polyphenols

2 tablespoons oats — slow-digesting carbs for steady energy

1 banana — fast carbs, potassium, smooth texture

¼ cup fat-free Greek yogurt (Chobani) — protein, creaminess, probiotics

¼ teaspoon Ceylon cinnamon — flavor plus potential blood sugar benefits

2 cups Fairlife fat-free milk — high protein, low sugar, lactose-free

What's intentionally not included:

No chia seeds

No fish oil

No peanuts

These fats slow digestion, so I save the peanuts for after the workout.

Macros:

Calories: ~456 Protein: ~37 g Carbs: ~76 g Fat: ~1.5 g

Fiber: ~10.5 g

Dinner: simple, structured, and repeatable

Dinner is where there's a little more variety—but not as much as you might think. Again, the idea is to keep it simple and reliable in terms of fueling and supporting optimal aging. Most meals are eaten at home because it's easier (and cheaper) to manage what goes into our food that way. Restaurant meals are often loaded with sodium, sugars, and fats to make them taste better.

Every dinner starts with:

2.5–3 cups of a garden salad blend, topped with cucumbers if available

1 tablespoon of extra-virgin olive oil

Optional: 1 tablespoon of guacamole or a few croutons (or both)

After the salad, the main plate follows a consistent pattern: a lean protein, a starch, and a vegetable.

A typical dinner might look like this:

4–5 ounces chicken breast

2–3 ounces (dry) pasta

A serving of broccoli

We generally use lean cuts of meat such as chicken breast, a baked pork chop, or baked fish such as cod. On rare occasions, we'll have red meat. The idea is to vary the ingredients while sticking to the general concept and keeping portion sizes reasonable.

Dinner might be followed by a small dessert, such as:

A small single serving of sherbet, or

A slice of my wife's angel food cake with her homemade low-sugar whipped cream and fresh fruit

A glass of Fairlife fat-free milk usually accompanies dinner.

We do have a Saturday night routine at a local barbecue restaurant. A typical meal there might be:

5–6 ounces pork barbecue (from the butt—lower fat)

A small serving of Brunswick stew

A small serving of field peas (a great source of protein)

When eating out for other reasons, we aim for mindful choices without obsessing over perfection.

Snacking: intentional, not mindless

Daily snacks include:

One apple between lunch and dinner

A handful of pistachios shared with our German Shepherd each evening

Occasional peanuts or cashews

Occasional cookies, eaten sparingly and intentionally

Apples — why "an apple a day" actually helps

An "apple a day" habit does real work for you:

Fiber: A medium apple has ~4 g of fiber, which helps with satiety, blood sugar control, and gut health.

Polyphenols: Apples contain antioxidants that may support cardiovascular health and reduce oxidative stress.

Low energy density: ~95 kcal for a decent volume of food — great for "filling, not heavy" snacking.

Chew time and ritual: It slows you down, gives a defined snack moment, and replaces more calorie-dense options.

It fits my whole philosophy: simple, repeatable, low-friction, and aligned with both health and weight management.

Fueling for workouts

Two staples make up almost all of my on-the-go workout fuel:

Clif Bar Crunchy Peanut Butter bars — durable, steady energy

Honey Stinger waffles — fast-digesting carbs for quick boosts

Clif Bars provide sustained energy; Honey Stingers provide rapid energy. Between the two, I can match the fuel to the effort.

Workout Fueling Calories

On workout days, I need to take in more calories. These aren't "snacks" in the casual sense — they're fuel. They're intentional, functional, and necessary if I want to train hard, recover well, and age optimally.

A typical 40-mile ride looks like this:

- ½ Clif Bar at mile 12
- ½ Clif Bar at mile 24
- (Total: 1 full Clif Bar — ~260 calories)
- 1 Honey Stinger waffle at mile 36
- (~150 calories)
- Post-workout handful of nuts
- (~170 calories)

That's ~580 additional calories on top of my normal daily pattern — and it's all by design. Fueling properly during and after workouts helps maintain energy, protect muscle, and support recovery. It's not "extra." It's part of the plan.

A Rough Macro & Calorie Analysis of a Typical Day

Below is an accurate breakdown of my daily intake — one table for workout days and one for non-workout days. These reflect what I actually eat, not an idealized version.

Workout Day Totals

Category	Calories	Protein	Carbs	Fat
Breakfast	~415	44 g	54 g	4-5 g
Lunch	~456	37 g	76 g	1.5 g
Dinner	~850	62 g	65 g	12 g
Normal Snacks	~325	7 g	25 g	14 g
Workout Fueling	~410	5 g	65 g	12 g
Post-Workout Nuts	~170	5 g	10 g	14 g
TOTAL	~2,626	160 g	295 g	57-58 g

Non-Workout Day Totals

Category	Calories	Protein	Carbs	Fat
Breakfast	~415	44 g	54 g	4-5 g
Lunch	~694	46 g	86 g	22 g
Dinner	~850	62 g	65 g	12 g
Normal Snacks	~325	7 g	25 g	14 g
TOTAL	~2,284	159 g	230 g	52-53 g

Important Protein Observation

Even with the additional workout-day fueling calories, my protein intake naturally stays in the optimal range for my weight — around 150–160 grams per day. That's almost exactly 1 gram per pound of bodyweight, which is the gold standard for maintaining muscle, supporting recovery, and aging well.

The structure does the work. The numbers simply follow.

Drinks

I keep beverages simple:

Water

Fairlife fat-free milk

Beetroot juice

No sodas, no coffee, no tea, no energy drinks.

Alcohol

Much has been written recently about alcohol and aging, and the trend is clear: more and more research suggests there may not be any "safe" amount of alcohol when it comes to long-term health.

I stopped drinking entirely in June of 2017, and two things drove that decision.

First, I had started using a Fitbit to monitor my sleep and recovery. It became obvious that even a single beer could wreck my sleep. Not just nudge it—wreck it. Once you see that pattern in your own data, it's hard to unsee.

Second, I walked alongside someone I care deeply about as they struggled with addiction, doing my best to support them at every step. But over time, that support began to feel hollow—I couldn't ignore the inauthenticity of encouraging their recovery while still engaging in drinking occasionally. That tension stayed with me until I finally faced it and chose to stop.

The benefits were immediate and undeniable:

No more empty calories

Better sleep

Better performance

Better relationships

Better self-respect

I haven't found a single compelling reason to start again.

Some longevity experts argue that alcohol can support social connection. I understand the sentiment, but I don't buy the premise. I still engage with the same people in the same environments—many of which involve alcohol—and I've never felt socially excluded or diminished by not drinking. In fact, several people in my circle have reduced or eliminated alcohol themselves.

It's not a popular idea, but it's worth asking yourself:
Why do I drink? What would life look like if I didn't?

For me, removing alcohol has been one of the highest-impact decisions I've made for my health and my aging. Alcohol contains empty calories that don't contribute to the intentional method for how I fuel for life.

Smoking

The evidence is clear. If you use tobacco in any form—smoking, vaping, chewing, snuff—stopping or reducing your use is one of the most powerful steps you can take toward aging well. This is low-hanging fruit on the road to optimal aging. Some reports even indicate that smoking prematurely ages the skin making one look up to 10 years older than their actual age. Your body and face will thank you for every reduction you make.

Chapter 3 Summary

You learned in this chapter that fueling your body intentionally is one of the most powerful levers you have for aging well. Your body is adaptable, but it can only compensate for so long when the inputs are poor. The goal isn't perfection — it's consistency, awareness, and simplicity.

Here are the core principles you can carry forward:

- You can't out-exercise a bad diet.
- Structure beats willpower.
- Daily weigh-ins reveal trends, not judgment.
- Ranges work better than targets.
- Consistency compounds.
- Small choices add up.
- Alcohol and tobacco are high-impact levers.

Your Turn

Choose one or two of these practices to begin — small steps create big momentum.

- Define your healthy weight range. Use the BMI chart as a starting point. Pick a midpoint and give yourself a ±5 lb. buffer. Track your weight daily — without judgment. Look for trends, not perfection.
- Simplify one meal. Create a "default meal" you can repeat 90% of the time.
- Audit your snacks. Replace one mindless snack with an intentional one.
- Evaluate your beverages. Eliminate anything that doesn't support your goals.
- Reflect on alcohol. Ask yourself: Why do I drink? What would life look like if I didn't?

The Law of Fuel is simple: What you put into your body determines what you can get out of it.

➤ IT'S NOT WHAT YOU KNOW, IT'S WHAT YOU DO. ➤

Fuel is only half of the equation. What you put in determines the quality of your energy — but what you do with that energy determines the quality of your life.

In the next chapter, we shift from input to output.
From fueling to burning.
From nutrition to movement.

CHAPTER 4 — THE LAW OF MOVEMENT: TRAIN FOR THE LONG GAME

The Law of Movement is simple: Your body adapts to what you ask of it.

When I first got serious about getting in shape, I didn't join a gym. I didn't hire a trainer. I didn't buy fancy equipment. I went upstairs to the bonus room above our garage and started with what I had: a few dumbbells, some old physical therapy stretches, and a determination to stop drifting.

My routine was simple — ten minutes of stretching, crunches, push-ups, bicep curls, and tricep presses. Nothing heroic. Nothing Instagram-worthy. But it was consistent. And consistency, as you've seen throughout this book, is the real superpower.

Over the years, that little routine made me modestly stronger. It wasn't transformative, but it was a start. It built competence. It built confidence. And it built a habit.

Then, about three years ago, something unexpected happened — one of those serendipitous moments that seems small at the time but ends up changing everything.

My next-door neighbor, who commutes to New York three days a week, stopped me after a bike ride. He asked me for a favor:

"Will you join my gym and be my workout buddy? I just need someone to make sure I go twice a week."

My first reaction was an immediate, polite no. I didn't want the hassle. I didn't want the schedule commitment. And honestly, I didn't want to go to a gym. I was comfortable in my little bonus-room bubble.

But the idea stuck with me. Maybe it was time to level up. Maybe my ten-minute routine had taken me as far as it could. Maybe I needed a nudge.

So I visited the gym. And knowing I'd have someone there who already knew the ropes made the decision easier. I signed up on the spot.

Three years later, I'm a reluctant gym rat — and grateful for it.

Why Strength Train?

You may be wondering why strength training matters so much — especially as we age. For me, the answer is simple: I want to take care of the people I love, both now and in the future. I want to be able to pick up my future grandchildren without worrying about throwing out my back. If life hands me a difficult season, I want the physical capacity to push a wheelchair for someone I care about.

And beyond that, I want to travel without relying on someone else to lift my bag into the overhead bin. I want to manage my weight more easily — and muscle is the metabolic engine that makes that possible. Losing 10% of your muscle mass every decade (sarcopenia) is not a fate I'm willing to accept. Strong muscles support strong bones, too. And if I'm being completely honest, I want to look good. There's nothing wrong with a little healthy vanity.

So. let's get into the nuts and bolts of what my program looks like now that I'm in the gym roughly every other day. My gym buddy joins me two or three times a week, and I supplement those sessions with solo visits — often with my wife and / or daughter, who decided to join in (and occasionally with both of them together).

Going to the gym turned out to be nothing like I expected. I had visions of sweaty gym bros grunting and slamming weights around. Instead, we joined a large chain gym (Planet Fitness) where that kind of behavior simply isn't part of the culture. The environment is welcoming, predictable, and surprisingly efficient.

We move through the gym with a semi-programmed plan. "Optimal" doesn't mean rigid — it means intentional. We go in knowing what we want to accomplish, and then we adapt based on what equipment is available. Each session includes at least ten exercises targeting specific muscle groups, all of which we can complete in 30 minutes or less. That usually leaves time for a short cardio finisher at the end (more on that later).

The key is recovery. Gains don't happen in the gym — they happen afterward, when the body adapts to the stress you applied. That's why we alternate muscle groups and avoid overworking the same areas on consecutive days.

Here are the last two sessions I completed this week on back-to-back days:

Wednesday — Upper Body Focus

- 10 overhand pull-ups
- 3 × 10 dips
- 10 palm-to-palm pull-ups
- 3 × 10 standing bicep curls
- 3 × 10 standing overhead tricep presses
- 3 × 10 incline bench press
- 3 × 10 dumbbell lateral raises
- 3 × 10 upright dumbbell rows
- 3 × 15 lateral horizontal cable cross pulls
- 3 × 15 cable shoulder cross raises
- 3 × 15 cable face pulls
- 1 × 25 ab-rack leg raises
- 10-minute uphill treadmill walk (15° incline)

All of that — including the treadmill — in under 45 minutes.

Thursday — Lower Body Focus

- 10 chin-ups (underhand grip)
- 3 × 10 dips
- 3 × 10 weighted step-ups (each leg)
- 3 × 10 leg extensions
- 3 × 10 leg curls
- 3 × 15 calf presses
- 3 × 10 hack squats
- 3 sets of Romanian deadlifts
- 1 × 25 shoulder shrugs
- 1 × 10 weighted Bulgarian split squats (each leg)
- 1 × 25 ab-rack leg lifts
- 10-minute uphill treadmill walk (15° incline)

Again — all completed in under 45 minutes.

Don't worry if some of these terms sound unfamiliar. I didn't know them either when I started. None of this is rocket science. These are basic, accessible movements that anyone can learn. I was fortunate to have a buddy who already knew the ropes, but even if you don't, most gyms offer free classes or one-on-one instruction. Gym intimidation doesn't need to be part of your story.

Here are the key takeaways from this schedule:

- Wednesday focused on upper body; Thursday focused on lower body. This alternation is intentional — recovery is essential for building muscle and preventing injury.
- Some exercises repeat, like pull-ups and ab work. That's intentional too.
- Nothing here is complicated. These movements are simple, learnable, and effective. The real key is proper form and choosing weights that challenge you without compromising technique.

Cardio

I strength train to avoid sarcopenia — the slow, steady loss of muscle mass that sneaks up on us as we age. Strength training is essential for keeping our skeletal muscles strong, but what about one of the most important muscles in the body — our heart?

That's where cardio comes in.

Heart disease is the number one cause of death. If we want to age well, we can't ignore the circulatory and respiratory systems that keep everything else running. When people ask me which is more important — strength training or cardio — my answer is simple:

Yes.

They work together. They support each other. You need both.

So what counts as cardio?

Anything that elevates your heart rate for a sustained period of time. Walking the dog? Absolutely. Vacuuming? Sure. Swimming, biking, dancing, jogging, walking the golf course instead of riding in a cart — all great. The key is finding what works for you and doing it consistently.

Since this book is about my playbook, let me show you what I do. Don't let it intimidate you — our bodies are built for movement, and most of us are capable of far more than we give ourselves credit for. And if you're reading this book, I'm guessing you're not aiming for an average life. You want to live optimally.

Let's get into it.

My Daily Foundation: The Dog Walk

Within the first hour of waking up, I try to triage my work responsibilities, get things under control, and then get outside for a few minutes. That means taking my dog for a brisk 30-minute walk.

But before we get into the specifics of that walk, we need to define a term that shows up a lot in my routine: Zone 2.

Zone 2

Zone 2 is simply a comfortable, steady pace where your heart is working but not struggling. You're breathing a little harder than normal, but you can still hold a conversation without gasping. Think of it as the "I could keep this up for a while" zone.

It's the sweet spot for building your aerobic engine — the part of your fitness that helps you burn fat efficiently, improve metabolic health, and increase endurance without beating up your joints or leaving you exhausted.

Here's how I think about Zone 2:

How Zone 2 Feels

- You can talk, but you wouldn't break into song.
- It feels steady, sustainable, and almost meditative.
- On a scale of 1–10, it's a 3 or 4 — not easy, not hard, just… steady.

How to Know You're There

- The talk test works surprisingly well.
- A heart-rate monitor helps if you want precision.
- For most people, Zone 2 is roughly 60–70% of max heart rate.

Why It Matters

Zone 2 training:

- Improves your ability to burn fat
- Builds more and healthier mitochondria (your cells' power plants)
- Improves insulin sensitivity
- Increases endurance
- Reduces stress and fatigue
- Is gentle enough to do frequently

The biggest mistake people make is going too fast. If you push too hard, you drift into Zone 3 — where you burn more sugar than fat and fatigue more quickly. Zone 2 is about patience, not speed.

Back to the Dog Walk

For me, a Zone 2 walk means keeping my heart rate around 103 beats per minute. Here's the math:

- 220 – my age (62) = 158
- 65% of 158 ≈ 103 BPM

Through trial and error (and a lot of dog walks), I've learned that I need to move at about 3 miles per hour to stay in that sweet spot.

But here's the thing about dog walking: the human may want to walk at 3 MPH… the dog may have other ideas.

My current dog — a beautiful 5-year-old long-haired German Shepherd — is all business. She keeps pace with me and seems to take personal responsibility for making sure I don't slack off.

My previous dog, a lovable golden retriever, had a very different philosophy. A 1.5-mile walk could easily turn into a 60-minute sniff-fest. Walking her was wonderful, but it wasn't cardio. So after our leisurely stroll, I'd drop her off at home and head back out for a second 30-minute Zone 2 walk.

Either way, the math is simple:

30 minutes × 7 days = 210 minutes of cardio per week.

Just like that, we're already in the minimum recommended range of 150–300 minutes per week.

But we're not aiming for minimums.

We're aiming for optimal.

Adding More Steady-State Cardio

In addition to the daily walks, I add more Zone 2 work through cycling — my favorite form of cardio. I've loved riding since I got my first tricycle. I don't enjoy stationary bikes, but put me outside in the fresh air and I'm happy.

I also prefer to avoid cars, so I ride on greenways and trails.

Several years ago, I started with short rides — a few miles at a time. I remember proudly telling my doctor that I was riding 12 miles a day.

Then I got more serious.

Three years ago, I logged 3,400 miles.

The next year, I ramped it up to 5,255 miles — 187 rides, averaging 28 miles each. That worked out to roughly every other day, contributing about 400 minutes of cardio per week.

That sounds like a lot — and it is. But here's the thing:

The average American adult watches 3.7 hours of TV per day.

We all have time. It's just a matter of how we choose to use it. And if you must watch TV, do it on a stationary bike and turn a sedentary habit into something that supports your health.

Pushing My Limits

Last year, I wanted to see what my body was truly capable of. I'm not a former college athlete. I don't have elite genetics. I'm just a regular 62-year-old guy who decided to test his limits.

I set a goal of 10,000 miles.

I hit it the Saturday after Thanksgiving and finished the year at 10,344 miles — 250 rides averaging 41.5 miles each. I did two rides over 100 miles (one was 114). Forty-two of my rides were over 62 miles — a metric century.

Do I recommend everyone do this?

No.

And I won't repeat it myself — I'm dialing back to a more sustainable 6,000 miles this year.

But I share this because I want you to see what's possible. Our bodies are capable of extraordinary things when we train them consistently and intelligently. If I can do it, you can to.

A Quick Myth-Buster

Some experts claim that high levels of cardio make it impossible to build muscle.

I'm living proof that this isn't necessarily true.

Last year, while riding over 10,000 miles, I lost 14 pounds of fat and gained 4 pounds of muscle — a net loss of 10 pounds. That's called body re-composition, and it's absolutely possible with the right balance of strength training, cardio, and nutrition.

HIIT (High-Intensity Interval Training)

If you read anything about fitness these days, you'll eventually run into the term HIIT — High-Intensity Interval Training. It's especially popular in conversations about improving VO_2 max, which is a measure of how well your body uses oxygen and is often considered one of the best overall indicators of fitness. We'll get into VO_2 max shortly, but for now, let's focus on what HIIT actually is and how it fits into my playbook.

HIIT is simple in concept: short bursts of very intense effort followed by periods of recovery. You push hard, then you back off. Heart rate up, heart rate down. Studies consistently show that HIIT is a powerful and efficient way to improve conditioning. And yes — it absolutely has a place in training for optimal aging, even for those of us with a little grey in our hair.

Most of my cardio is steady-state Zone 2 work — my daily walks and my bike rides. But I do mix in a little HIIT as well. You may remember that I finish each strength-training session with a 10-minute treadmill session. Usually that's a moderate uphill walk. But once a week, I change things up and do a 10-minute HIIT run.

Here's what that looks like:

- I start with a one-minute walk.
- Then I jog lightly for another minute at around 5 MPH.
- Then the fun begins. I ramp the treadmill up to 10–10.5 MPH and run hard for 30–45 seconds.
- After that interval, I drop back down to a fast walk — around 3.5 MPH — and watch my heart rate.

- When my heart rate drops about 30 beats per minute from its peak, I start the next fast-run interval.

In a typical 10-minute session, I get through about three cycles and always finish with a walking cool-down.

I also sprinkle in a little HIIT on the bike. There are sections of my route that naturally lend themselves to a sprint, followed by a recovery stretch. I might only do one of these per ride — and I certainly don't do them every ride. HIIT is intense. A little goes a long way.

Is my strategy effective?

My VO_2 max seems to think so.

We'll dig into the details soon, but here's a teaser: despite the common belief that VO_2 max inevitably declines with age, mine has actually increased over the last three years since I started tracking it.

How to Get Started

Hopefully, by now I've encouraged you to want to get moving — and to move heavy things. But where do you begin?

First, make sure your body is ready for the challenge. This may include a visit with your primary medical provider to confirm that you're cleared to start a fitness program. I'm not a physician, and I'm certainly not your physician. I can't guarantee that the routines I've described are appropriate for you. Please take this step so you're starting from a safe, informed baseline.

Next, plan on starting slowly. As the saying goes, you need to walk before you can run — and in this case, that may be literally true. When our kids were young and faced with a big task, we used to ask them, "How do you eat an elephant?" They'd roll their eyes and answer, "One bite at a time." Most exercise programs fall apart because people try to take on too much too quickly. Baby steps, done with intention, are the way forward. One bite at a time.

I didn't start out doing sets of ten pull-ups at the gym. I didn't attempt my first 100-mile bike ride until years of riding experience. You don't need to start big. You just need to start.

Decide how you want to begin. I started at home with a few dumbbells, bodyweight exercises, and stretches. You can even improvise with soup cans. Walking is a fantastic entry point — accessible, gentle, and effective.

If you can find a buddy to join you, even better. Accountability becomes easier, and the whole experience becomes more enjoyable. If you're even a little competitive, you may find yourself pushing harder with a partner than you would alone.

If you choose to join a gym, visit several in your area. Start with the one closest to home — removing barriers is key. Many gyms offer beginner programs and classes for all levels. I joined the same gym my neighbor belonged to, and the 15-minute carpool ride gives us time to catch up. My membership allows access to any of their locations worldwide, and I've visited more than ten so far. It's a great way to stay consistent while traveling. A quick tip – if you are new to weightlifting, the machines at the gym are a great way to start rather than heading over to the racks of free weights. Once set up to fit you (a matter of a few seconds) the machines help to enforce proper movement and remove the necessity to not only move the weight but to also stabilize it as in the case of free weights. This can help to reduce the potential for injury significantly. transitioning to free weights can come later with experience and "grooving" of the movements. This is exactly the way I did it – and I didn't rush it. Even after three years in the gym, I still make use of some of the machines for some exercises. My wife has some instability in her neck. Her medical provider actually prescribed certain exercises that she should only do on machines to avoid potential issues. Another good reason to keep your medical provider in-the loop with what we are doing. It is always preferable to avoid issues rather than needing to fix them after the fact.

The important thing is to begin. And if you already have a baseline routine, consider how to elevate it — safely, effectively, and efficiently — to move from "good enough" to optimal.

How to Stay Motivated

Let me share a story from more than twenty years ago. Both of our kids were Suzuki Method violinists, starting at age four. A core concept of the Suzuki approach is the "Suzuki Triangle," where the teacher, the parent, and the student each form one side of an isosceles triangle — all equally important. Weekly lessons were followed by daily practice assignments, and the parent's job was to ensure that practice actually happened.

As you might imagine, getting a four-year-old to practice violin every day can feel like a Herculean task. After yet another lesson where the previous week's material hadn't improved much, I had an epiphany. The problem wasn't the kids' motivation. They loved playing. The problem was me.

When they asked, "Do we have to practice today," it was far too easy for me to think, "I'm tired… we'll just do more tomorrow," and give them the day off. Once I realized where the real breakdown was happening, the solution became obvious.

I told the kids we were changing the rules. From that day forward, we were going to practice every single day — no exceptions. That meant taking violins on vacation, squeezing in a quick session late at night, or practicing for just five minutes if that's all we could manage. And guess what? Once excuses were off the table, the kids practiced joyfully (well… mostly joyfully) for an entire year without missing a single day. Their progress skyrocketed.

You can probably see where I'm going with this.

If you set the expectation that you will move your body every single day — without exception — the internal debate disappears. On busy days, you can sprinkle in "exercise snacks": small, easy bursts of movement. I keep a grip-strength trainer on my desk and use it while on calls. But I strongly recommend planning your workouts in advance. If they're on your calendar, they're far more likely to happen.

Each week, my gym buddy and I coordinate our gym days around his travel schedule. That gives me a template for planning my bike rides. You'll find endless debates online about whether to do cardio or strength training first. My answer is always the same:

Yes.

Just do both. We're training for life, not the Olympics. (If you are training for the Olympics, feel free to ignore this advice and fine-tune your schedule.)

And yes — consider an exercise buddy. I've mentioned this before because it works. The only reason I ever joined a gym was because my neighbor needed a partner. It changed everything.

Working out at home is convenient, but it comes with distractions: doorbells, phone calls, spouses needing help. At the gym, I'm there for one purpose. It's easy to stay focused. Our sessions are efficient and productive. We walk in with a plan (which we adjust based on equipment availability) and get it done.

And the variety of equipment is hard to match at home. Machines require almost no setup. Free weights are available in every imaginable size. Moving from one exercise to the next is as simple as walking a few steps. It's a friction-free environment for getting stronger.

Goal Setting

We'll talk more about goal-setting later in the book, but I want to give you a few examples of how goals have accelerated my own progress.

When I agreed to join the gym with my workout buddy, I told him I had one condition: we needed a goal. After our first month of workouts, we decided on a big one — being able to perform three sets of ten pull-ups within four months.

If you've ever attempted pull-ups, you know how ambitious this is. Pull-ups are a classic "compound exercise," meaning they work multiple muscle groups at once. They're brutally honest. You can't fake a pull-up.

So how did we start?

Our gym has an assisted pull-up machine — a brilliant piece of equipment that lets you offset some of your bodyweight. You still perform the movement with perfect form, but you can choose how much weight to "make disappear." We began with a 60-pound offset.

Every gym visit, we checked in on that machine first. Once we could do three sets of ten at 60 pounds of assistance, we reduced the offset by 10 pounds. Then again. And again. Eventually, we reached our goal: three sets of ten on the bare bar, no assistance.

It took four months — exactly what we planned — and hitting that milestone was incredibly motivating.

And here's an important point: celebrate your victories, even the small ones. Walk a half-mile farther than you ever have? Fantastic. Build on it. Momentum matters.

In our case, pull-ups became our warm-up for every gym visit. And I'll admit — I love the look on the younger guys' faces when the "old guy" hops up and knocks out a clean set.

After celebrating our first victory, we needed a new challenge. We settled on a sprint triathlon — the shortest distance typically offered. We found a local event with a 250-yard swim, a 10-mile bike ride, and a 2-mile run.

Our mission was set.

Neither of us were strong swimmers. In fact, my buddy had a traumatic experience as a kid when he was caught in a rip tide and had to be revived. Agreeing to the swim portion was a major leap for him.

But we slowly adjusted our self-images. We weren't just two guys trying to complete a triathlon. We were becoming triathletes. That identity shift made the training easier to commit to.

Every week, we added structured training to our routine:

- time in the pool,
- treadmill or outdoor runs,
- and hours on the bike riding the greenways.

After several months, we could say it with confidence:

We were triathletes.

Chapter 4 Summary: The Law of Movement

Movement is the foundation of vitality. In this chapter, we explored the full spectrum of what it means to train for the long game — not as an athlete chasing medals, but as a human being

Strength Training

- Build and maintain muscle
- Protect against sarcopenia
- Support metabolic health
- Train 2–3× per week
- Use simple, repeatable movements
- Progress load gradually

Zone 2 Cardio

- Steady, conversational-pace effort
- Improve fat metabolism and endurance
- Strengthen aerobic engine
- Minimum: 150–300 minutes per week
- Optimal: go beyond the minimum (walks + rides + daily movement)
- Use sustainable activities (walking, cycling, swimming)
- Keep intensity low and consistent

HIIT

- Short bursts of high intensity
- Boost VO_2 max and cardiovascular capacity

- Use sparingly — 1× per week is enough
- Alternate hard intervals with full recovery
- Keep sessions brief (5–10 minutes)

Getting Started

- Begin safely — confirm medical readiness
- Start small and progress gradually – one bite at a time
- Remove barriers (location, equipment, time)
- Use simple tools: bodyweight, dumbbells, walking
- Focus on consistency over intensity

Staying Motivated

- Plan workouts in advance
- Move daily — eliminate the internal debate
- Use "exercise snacks" on busy days
- Leverage accountability (buddy, gym environment)
- Use music, cues, and routines to stay engaged
- Create a distraction-free training space

Goal Setting

- Set clear, measurable targets
- Break goals into small, achievable steps
- Track progress regularly
- Celebrate small wins
- Let identity evolve with capability ("I am an athlete")

Your Turn

Here are a few simple ways to put the Law of Motion into action:

- Choose Your Strength Routine. Pick 6–10 basic movements you can perform safely. Commit to doing them 2–3 times per week. Keep it simple. Keep it consistent.
- Establish a Daily Zone 2 Habit. Start with a 20–30 minute brisk walk. Use the talk test. If you can speak in full sentences but wouldn't break into song, you're there.
- Add One HIIT Session Per Week. Just one. Short, sharp, and controlled. A little goes a long way.
- Track Something. Heart rate, steps, miles, minutes — it doesn't matter. What gets measured gets reinforced.
- Revisit Your Identity. Instead of saying "I'm trying to exercise more," try: "I'm someone who moves every day." Identity drives behavior.

The Law of Movement is simple: Your body adapts to what you ask of it.

Ask consistently. Ask wisely. Ask more than the minimum.

➤ IT'S NOT WHAT YOU KNOW, IT'S WHAT YOU DO. ➤

Movement is essential — but it's only half the equation.

The other half happens when you're not moving.

Your body doesn't get stronger during the workout. It gets stronger during the recovery. Your heart adapts at rest. Your muscles rebuild at rest. Your brain resets at rest. And nothing accelerates or sabotages your progress more than the quality of your sleep.

So now that we've built your movement playbook, it's time to explore the quieter, often overlooked side of optimal aging — the Law of Restoration.

Next up: Chapter 5 — Sleep & Recovery.

CHAPTER 5 — THE LAW OF RESTORATION: SLEEP & RECOVERY

The Law of Restoration is simple: When you recover well, you realize the gains from your efforts — and that's what allows optimal aging.

You can train hard, eat well, and push your body to impressive places — but without restoration, none of it sticks. The real magic of aging well doesn't happen during the workout; it happens in the quiet hours afterward, when your body repairs, rebuilds, and resets. Sleep is the master lever of that process. Recovery is the multiplier. Together, they determine whether your efforts compound or collapse. If the Law of Motion is about asking more of your body, the Law of Restoration is about giving it the space to answer.

Sleep isn't passive downtime. It's an active, highly coordinated biological repair cycle. Muscles rebuild. Hormones rebalance. The brain clears waste, consolidates memory, and resets emotional circuits. Miss that cycle, and everything else becomes harder.

I didn't always appreciate how central sleep was to my health. For years, I treated it like a negotiable luxury — something I could trim when life got busy. That changed when I started wearing my Fitbit around the clock and could finally see what was happening. I've already mentioned how alcohol wrecked my sleep, but that was only the beginning. I began correlating how I felt — physically, mentally, emotionally — with my sleep score, especially my deep sleep and REM sleep. Once I saw the pattern, I started protecting my sleep the way my German Shepherd protects her bones.

One of the most comprehensive and readable books I've found on the topic is Shawn Stevenson's *Sleep Smarter*. He outlines 21 strategies to optimize sleep — which sounds a lot like what we're trying to do here: age optimally. I've implemented many of his strategies and now have a robust sleep-hygiene system. Here's what my sleep playbook looks like.

A good night's sleep actually starts first thing in the morning. I've already mentioned how I make every effort to get outside with my pup for a morning walk. That's not just about getting a jump on the day's cardio — it's far more important. Morning sunlight resets the body's circadian rhythm. Without getting too deep into the weeds, light signals the pineal gland to stop producing melatonin and kick-start the wakefulness cycle. Step one, complete.

Next is the sleep environment. It seems obvious, but a dark, quiet room is essential. The question is: how dark? Andrew Huberman addressed this in one of his podcasts — it turns out it doesn't take much light at all to disrupt sleep. Just a few lux (the equivalent of a moonlit night) between 10 p.m. and 4 a.m. can have negative effects. Huberman also cited a study in which even light at a relatively low 100 lux could still penetrate the eyelids. We already had room-darkening shades, but between the alarm clock display, the cable box, and the LED on the TV, our room was bright enough to read by.

So I took three actions:

1. I dimmed the alarm clock to the lowest visible setting.

2. I covered the cable box display with electrical tape.

3. I bought a sleep mask and now wear it every night.

The remaining light from the TV is just enough to navigate to the bathroom safely without turning on overhead lights — a reasonable compromise.

Temperature matters too. My wife and I experimented and found that 68 degrees is our sweet spot. And while it seems obvious, a comfortable bed is non-negotiable. We learned this firsthand when we replaced our old, worn-out mattress with a new one — a true game changer. Don't try to squeeze extra years out of a mattress that's past its prime.

Now that we've started our day with early-morning sun exposure and created a comfortable environment in which to retire, it's time to prepare ourselves. My routine is built on consistency.

First, I make sure to allow at least three hours between dinner and bedtime to give digestion time to run its course. For me, that means starting dinner around 5:00 p.m. The only food I have afterward is the handful of pistachios my pup and I share around 8:00 (she tends to get most of them). As I mentioned earlier, I don't use caffeine — it triggers migraines — so that's not a factor for me. But for others, stopping caffeinated drinks in the afternoon (the earlier the better) is the way to go. And alcohol? Not even a consideration. One beer and I can kiss a good night's sleep goodbye.

Next, I turn my attention to blue light exposure. Common advice is to limit blue light after sunset. Besides the sun itself, where does blue light come from? LED and fluorescent lights — and digital screens. In a perfect world, we'd all put our phones away, turn off our laptops and tablets, and shut down the TV after dark. In today's world, that's not realistic for most households. My compromise is to switch to blue-blocking glasses after sunset. Do they work? The evidence isn't rock-solid, but they probably don't hurt. (I wouldn't wear them during daylight hours — we want blue light then to help shut off melatonin production.) I asked my eye doctor about this. His take: if you need to wear glasses anyway, they might as well be blue-blocking at night. One thing I never, ever do is take my phone into the bedroom.

I also try to give my mind a break from anything stimulating. That means no late-night work on the computer, where things can get a little too activating. No intense TV shows or books that could spike anxiety. Nighttime is zen time. About an hour before bed, I take a small amount of magnesium citrate. It relaxes my muscles and helps me fall asleep — and it has other benefits I'll address later.

Consistency also applies to timing. I aim for a 10:00 p.m. lights-out curfew and a 6:00 a.m. wake-up. That may vary by fifteen minutes either way, but circadian rhythm thrives on regularity and predictable light cues. Our bodies don't care what day of the week it is — so I keep the same schedule every day.

All of these habits work synergistically to improve my sleep, but one of the biggest effects I saw came from using a sleep mask. I collected data for several months and saw a 7% improvement in my sleep score after implementing the mask. That is significant. My advice: if you don't currently wear a sleep mask, give one a try.

Red Light Therapy and HRV: A Surprising Boost to Recovery

I stumbled into red light therapy almost by accident. While traveling in Denver, I visited a Planet Fitness near my hotel. This particular location had a "Total Body Enhancement" machine — a booth that combines red light exposure with a vibrating platform. It wasn't UV light like a tanning bed; it was safe for skin and marketed as having potential benefits for recovery, skin health, and overall well-being. I was curious, so I stepped in for the standard 12-minute session.

It was surprisingly pleasant — bright but not overwhelming, with gentle vibration and ambient music. I didn't think much of it at the time. But when I got home and checked my Fitbit HRV trends, something caught my attention. My HRV distribution had shifted upward. We'll discuss HRV in depth later, but for now, just know that heart rate variability is a measure of how adaptable your body is to the demands placed on it — a powerful indicator of recovery and readiness. My local gym didn't have the same machine, but another location a few minutes farther down the road did, so I started using it a couple of times per week.

The data trends got my analytical brain firing. I exported my HRV data and compared the 45 days before I started using the machine to the 45 days after. The result: a 10% increase in HRV. That's not a small change — especially for a metric as sensitive and multifactorial as HRV.

Was it the red light? The vibration? A placebo effect? Coincidence? I didn't want to jump to conclusions, so I dug deeper.

I found a book by Dave Maxfield called *Up Your HRV*, which referenced a study led by Dr. Paul Gourion-Arseneault and published in Frontiers in Physiology. The researchers found that HRV increased significantly during exposure to red light. That was enough to make me take the possibility seriously.

Andrew Huberman has also discussed research showing that light therapy can improve visual acuity — especially when exposure happens within a few hours of waking. That caught my attention because the morning I shot my best sporting clays score of the year, I had gotten up early and used the red-light machine before heading to the range.

It seemed there was something to the technology — but I was getting tired of driving to the alternate gym location. So I did some research and invested in my own panel to use at home. The first one I bought was a tabletop-sized model from Mitoredlight. I keep it under my desk and use it daily, targeting my legs in a single 10-minute session each morning. It might be a placebo effect, but my knees have never been happier. And while the research is still in its early stages, I'm not the only one doing this. Plenty of professional and collegiate sports teams have adopted red light treatment as a recovery tool.

Since the panel is portable, I can move it around to treat whatever areas might need attention in addition to my daily leg session. I even picked up a vibration plate so I can simulate the machine setup from the gym. Red light has become a consistent part of my recovery plan.

Because I travel frequently, I wanted a way to take red light with me. I purchased a rechargeable portable unit from the same company. I use that at home too — especially before sporting clays tournaments — to jump-start my visual acuity. I don't look directly into the red-light source; instead, I turn it on and let my eyes gaze over the light so I get indirect exposure. A session only takes two minutes.

And yes — next time you're in your dermatologist's office, check how much they charge for a red-light therapy session. Many use it as a cosmetic tool for the face and even for encouraging hair growth.

For me, red light therapy became another tool in my recovery toolbox — not a magic bullet, but a meaningful contributor to better HRV, better readiness, and better performance. And as I've learned throughout this journey, anything that nudges HRV upward tends to nudge everything else in the right direction too.

Earthing

Red light therapy taught me something important about recovery: sometimes the body responds to inputs we don't fully understand yet. When I see a measurable improvement — especially in something as sensitive as HRV — I pay attention. That mindset opened the door to another practice I had once dismissed as fringe: earthing, or grounding. The idea sounds almost too simple — connecting your body directly to the earth — but like red light, it's one of those recovery tools where the early research is intriguing, and my own experience has been surprisingly positive. So I decided to run the same experiment-driven approach: try it, track it, and see if it moves the needle.

The easiest way to try earthing is to take your shoes and socks off and walk on bare ground. I have just finished reading Dick Van Dyke's book *100 Rules for Living to 100*, and guess what — that's exactly what he does. I'm not saying that's why he made it to the century mark, but this strategy has a surprising following. Proponents of earthing claim benefits such as:

- Reduction of inflammation and pain
- Improved sleep and stress reduction
- Cardiovascular and blood-flow improvements (including HRV)
- Increased energy and improved mood

- Immune system support
- Metabolic effects

Unfortunately, the existing research on earthing is sparse, and what does exist would not be considered rigorous by academic standards. So I put on my experimenter's white coat and got to work.

My Fitbit collects HRV data at night when the wearer is still, but I needed a device that could measure HRV on demand during the day. I purchased an armband heart-rate monitor for this purpose. Then I devised a simple experiment: collect HRV data while insulated from the ground by my shoes, and then again while barefoot on the earth.

I'd love to tell you I saw a huge difference — but I didn't. No immediate impact. But that's not always how physiology works. You don't build a bicep after a single gym session; sometimes gains accumulate slowly.

So I dug deeper.

I decided to "take one for the team" and buy a grounding pad. A grounding pad is a conductive flexible mat with a wire that connects to the ground terminal of a home electrical outlet. No current flows through it — a resistor is used for safety — but it brings the electrical potential of the earth into your home. Mine sits under my desk next to my red-light panel. I simply rest my bare feet on it while I work.

While I didn't see the same dramatic HRV increase I saw with red light therapy, I did notice something over time. I started this experiment in early 2022, during the downward trend of the COVID epidemic in the U.S. Four years later, I haven't had so much as a sniffle or a cold. Could this be the result of grounding improving immune support? Hard to say. But the investment was tiny, the barrier to use is low, and the risk is negligible. (I don't use the mat during thunderstorms.)

Some proponents of grounding even connect their beds to improve sleep. That might be an area I experiment with in the future.

For now, earthing has earned a place in my recovery routine — not because it produced a dramatic HRV spike, but because over time it seems to support the quiet, foundational systems that keep me healthy. And in the Law of Restoration, those small, steady nudges often matter more than the big swings.

Managing Exertion: The Hidden Power of Rest Days

One of the biggest lessons I've learned on this journey is that recovery isn't something you squeeze in around the edges of training — it is training. You can push hard, lift heavy, and rack up miles, but if you never give your body space to absorb the work, you're not getting stronger. You're just getting tired.

We tend to celebrate effort and intensity. Rest, on the other hand, can feel like weakness or lost progress. But the truth is simple: adaptation happens on the days you don't train. Muscles repair. Tendons remodel. Hormones rebalance. The nervous system resets. Skip that process long enough, and your body will force the issue with fatigue, irritability, poor sleep, or injury.

I've learned to treat rest days with the same respect I give my workouts. They're not optional. They're not "days off." They're part of the plan — the part that allows everything else to work.

Before we go further, it's time to get a little more scientific about HRV, because it's the key player in the recovery scene. WebMD describes HRV as "a measure of how much your heartbeat varies over time. A higher HRV is associated with better health and well-being, as it reflects the ability of your parasympathetic nervous system to regulate your heart rate and cope with stress." HRV measures the variation between successive heartbeats (in milliseconds) — not to be confused with your actual heart rate.

If your heart beats at 60 beats per minute — one beat per second — HRV tells you how much variation there is in that one-second interval. One beat might be 1.01 seconds apart, the next 0.95 seconds. That variability reflects how well your autonomic nervous system (ANS) is fine-tuning performance. We like to imagine our heartbeat as a metronome, steady and consistent, but that's not how a healthy system works. The vagus nerve plays a major role in this fine-tuning, helping the ANS balance recovery and readiness.

The ANS handles all the bodily functions we don't consciously think about — breathing, blood pressure, digestion, and preparing to respond to threats. It has two branches: the parasympathetic nervous system, responsible for relaxation and recovery, and the sympathetic nervous system, responsible for "fight or flight." HRV tells us how well these two systems are balanced. Higher HRV means the scales tip toward the parasympathetic side; lower HRV means stress, exertion, or illness may be at play.

So how do I know when I need to back off? Two ways — one high-tech, one high-touch.

In the next chapter, we'll get into the weeds on how I use wearable technology to improve performance, but that same technology helps me recognize when it's time to ease up. A quick glance at the app on my phone tells me if I'm on the verge of overdoing it. The tech provides a recommendation based on HRV, sleep, and cardio-load data — but it's still up to me to decide what to do with that information.

That's where the high-touch side comes in. Your body will tell you when it's time to slow down — if you're willing to listen. The magic happens when you merge the two systems. The tech can provide a helpful reminder, especially when your mind doesn't want to hear it. But I always grant my body and mind veto power over the tech. If the app says "go" and my body says "no," I listen to my body.

Slowing down doesn't necessarily mean spending the day on the couch. In fact, I find that gentle movement — walking the dog, for example — can aid recovery. I also like to get out on the bike the day after a long or intense ride just to get the legs moving and the blood flowing. Nothing intense — the kind of ride you'd take with your grandkids. And if you recall the workout examples in Chapter 4, those were done on successive days but focused on different muscle groups. Alternating muscle groups with a couple of days between working the same areas goes a long way toward preventing overuse and injury.

A partial deload can be helpful too — and by that, I mean reducing the lifting load a little. I do this when my HRV indicates some stress, my lifts seem to have plateaued, or when I'm just feeling a little fatigued. In these cases, I don't take days off — instead, I change up my weight and the number of reps. I might even cut the weight load in half. As an example, say I'm doing 3 sets of 10 reps on the leg extension machine. This machine works the quads on the front of the thigh — the dominant muscles that propel me on the bike. It's one of my favorites, and I'm able to push a lot of weight — say 245 pounds for the 3×10 session. Under a deload scenario, I might drop the weight to 125 pounds but increase the reps from 10 to 15. This gets the blood pumping and creates a nice feeling of recovery. I usually find I'm ready to push harder the next time I work the quads again.

Then there are the times when you take a full holiday from activity… — a few days or even a week. I don't do this often, but an occasional total break can be rejuvenating. My experience has shown that I often find a new gear I forgot I had when I return to the gym or the bike after an intentional break. These breaks aren't excuses to skip workouts. They're planned, thoughtful pauses taken by design. I schedule them when we have guests visiting, when we're traveling and workouts aren't convenient, or after a period of intense training like preparing for a major competition. These periods are good for the body — and just as importantly, good for the brain.

The Brain Needs Recovery Too: Meditation, Breathwork, and Stress Reset

Physical recovery is only half the story. The brain — with its constant stream of thoughts, decisions, emotions, and reactions — needs recovery just as much as the body does. Chronic stress, rumination, and mental overload drain the same systems that support physical performance. They suppress HRV, disrupt sleep, impair focus, and make even simple tasks feel harder. If the Law of Motion is about challenging the body, and the Law of Nutrition is about fueling it, then the Law of Restoration is about creating the conditions for both the body and the brain to come back stronger.

Over the past few years, I've learned that mental recovery isn't abstract or mystical. It's trainable. It's measurable. And it's accessible to anyone willing to practice. Meditation, breathwork, and intentional downshifting have become essential tools in my recovery system — not because I'm trying to become a monk, but because they help me show up calmer, clearer, and more resilient.

Meditation: Training the Mind Like a Muscle

I'll be honest: I was skeptical of meditation at first. It felt like "woo-hoo" territory — something other people did, not me. But I kept hearing about its benefits, especially for athletes and high performers, so I gave it a try. Today, I've logged almost 14,000 minutes of meditation using my MUSE device — an app with guided meditations paired with an EEG headset that provides quantitative feedback — and meditation has become a steady part of my routine.

In the beginning, I used MUSE every single day, building a streak of 216 consecutive sessions (remember the lesson from my kids' violin practice?). MUSE taught me how to practice mindfulness. Now, I use the device when I feel I need some remedial work or when I simply want to enjoy a guided session. Most days, I rely on the meditation "snacks" and breathwork techniques I developed during my training.

Mindfulness is often misunderstood. It's not about emptying your mind or shutting off thoughts. It's about paying attention on purpose, in the present moment, without judgment. Thoughts will come — that's what the mind does. The practice is noticing them and gently returning your attention to your breath or your anchor point. That's the rep. That's the training.

Meditation improves focus, emotional regulation, and stress resilience. It helps you stay grounded when life gets chaotic. It strengthens what psychologists call "attentional control," which is a fancy way of saying you can choose where your mind goes instead of being dragged around by it. And from a recovery standpoint, meditation nudges the nervous system toward parasympathetic dominance — the same state associated with higher HRV, better sleep, and improved readiness.

One of my favorite concepts is the "beginner's mind" — approaching each moment with curiosity rather than judgment. It's a powerful mindset for aging well. It keeps you adaptable, open, and willing to learn.

One of my favorite mediations is a "walking meditation". Simply go for a walk and let your attention shift to one sense. I like to listen for every sound I can detect. Birds chirping, a dog barking in the distance, my feet contacting the ground, a plane far overhead. I listen for the most subtle sounds as well as most obvious. Give it a try.

Breathwork: The Fastest Way to Shift the Nervous System

If meditation is strength training for the mind, breathwork is the quick-access reset button. It's portable, free, and works in under a minute. Breathwork is one of the fastest ways to influence HRV because it directly affects the vagus nerve — the main pathway of the parasympathetic nervous system.

Simple techniques like box breathing, extended-exhale breathing, or even slow nasal breathing can calm the body almost instantly. I've used breathwork before competitions, during stressful moments, and even when I feel my mind starting to spiral. It's a way to interrupt the stress response and bring the system back into balance.

For people who struggle with meditation, breathwork is often the gateway. It gives you something concrete to focus on, and the physiological effects are immediate. If this topic is of interest to you, pick up a copy of James Nestor's book *Breathe*. I did.

Box Breathing: The Reset Button

Box breathing deserves its own spotlight. Used by military operators, first responders, and elite athletes, it's one of the most reliable ways to regain control under pressure. The pattern is simple:

- Inhale for four seconds
- Hold for four
- Exhale for four
- Hold for four

Repeat for a minute or two.

This technique lowers heart rate, reduces anxiety, and sharpens focus. I've used it in high-pressure situations — on the range, before presentations, and even during moments of frustration — and it never fails to bring me back to center. It's the mental equivalent of tapping the brakes and regaining traction.

Quieting the Mind Under Pressure

The mind has a tendency to catastrophize. It jumps to worst-case scenarios, replays mistakes, and spins stories that have nothing to do with reality. Under pressure, this can derail performance faster than any physical limitation.

Meditation and breathwork interrupt that spiral. They create space between stimulus and response — a moment where you can choose how to react instead of being swept away by emotion. Over time, this becomes a trainable skill. You learn to recover mentally as deliberately as you recover physically.

Stress Reduction: Creating Space for the Brain to Downshift

Chronic stress is one of the biggest threats to recovery. It keeps the sympathetic nervous system stuck in overdrive, suppresses HRV, disrupts sleep, and drains energy. The brain needs intentional downshifting — moments of quiet, stillness, and presence — to reset.

For me, that means:

- short meditation sessions
- breathwork throughout the day
- quiet walks with my pup without my phone
- stepping away from screens
- giving myself permission to pause

These aren't luxuries. They're part of the recovery plan. They're the mental equivalent of rest days — the practices that allow the brain to repair, reorganize, and return stronger.

Chapter 5 Summary

This chapter explored the many layers of recovery — from sleep to cellular repair to nervous-system reset — and how each one contributes to readiness, resilience, and long-term health.

Sleep is the master lever. It's the foundation of physical and cognitive recovery, hormone regulation, memory consolidation, and emotional stability.

1. Sleep Hygiene Essentials
    - Keep a consistent bedtime and wake time
    - Make your room cool, dark, and quiet
    - Limit screens and bright light before bed
    - Avoid heavy meals and alcohol late in the evening
    - Use a wind-down routine to signal your brain it's time to sleep
    - Get morning sunlight exposure to anchor your circadian rhythm
2. Red light therapy can nudge HRV upward and support cellular repair, visual acuity, and readiness — a small but meaningful tool in your recovery toolbox.
3. Earthing may not produce immediate HRV spikes, but it offers low-risk, low-effort benefits that may support immune function, calm, and long-term well-being.
4. Rest days and deloads are not signs of weakness — they're where adaptation happens. Muscles repair, tendons remodel, hormones rebalance, and the nervous system resets.
5. HRV is your dashboard. It reflects the balance between stress and recovery and helps you know when to push and when to back off.

6. Meditation and breathwork train the brain the same way workouts train the body. They improve focus, emotional regulation, and stress resilience while nudging the nervous system toward parasympathetic dominance.
7. Intentional downshifting — quiet walks, screen breaks, mindful pauses — gives the brain the space it needs to reset and return stronger.

Recovery isn't passive. It's a skill — and like any skill, it gets stronger with practice.

Your Turn

Here are simple, practical ways to put the Law of Restoration into action. Start small by selecting one or two to experiment with:

1. Protect Your Sleep

- Set a consistent bedtime and wake time
- Keep your room cool, dark, and quiet
- Limit screens and bright light in the hour before bed

2. Try Red Light Therapy

- Use a panel or gym device for 5–10 minutes in the morning
- Avoid looking directly into the light
- Track your HRV for a few weeks to see if it helps

3. Experiment With Earthing

- Walk barefoot on grass or soil for a few minutes
- Try a grounding pad under your desk
- Notice how your body and mood respond over time

4. Schedule Rest Days

- Build at least one rest day into your weekly routine
- Use gentle movement — walking, light cycling — to aid recovery
- Consider a deload week after intense training blocks

5. Track Your HRV

- Use your wearable to monitor trends, not single numbers
- Let HRV guide your training intensity
- Listen to your body even when the tech says "go"

6. Practice Meditation

- Start with 3–5 minutes a day
- Use guided sessions or a device like MUSE
- Focus on consistency, not perfection

7. Use Breathwork as a Reset

- Try box breathing for one minute
- Use extended exhales to calm the system

- Practice before stressful events or competitions

8. Build Daily Downshifts

- Take short breaks from screens
- Go for quiet walks
- Give yourself permission to pause

Small, consistent recovery practices compound over time. They help you show up stronger, calmer, and more capable — not just in training, but in every part of life.

The Law of Restoration is simple: When you recover well, you realize the gains from your efforts — and that's what allows optimal aging.

➤ IT'S NOT WHAT YOU KNOW, IT'S WHAT YOU DO. ➤

PART II SUMMARY — Turning Intention into Action

Part II has been about the daily practices that determine how you feel, how you function, and how you age. These three laws — Fuel, Movement, and Restoration — form the physical core of an optimal life. Fuel gives your body the raw materials it needs to perform. Movement keeps you strong, capable, and adaptable. Restoration repairs the systems that make progress possible.

When these laws work together, your body stops being something you manage and becomes something you trust. You think more clearly. You move with more confidence. You recover with more resilience. You begin to feel the compounding effect of small, consistent choices — the kind of choices that turn intention into action and action into momentum.

Now that you've built the physical foundation that supports your goals, you're ready for the next step: learning to measure what matters. Part III is where your habits meet your data — where numbers, trends, and feedback loops help you refine your approach, sharpen your decisions, and experiment your way toward a stronger, longer life.

PART III — THE NUMBERS

You've now built the foundation: purpose, nutrition, movement, and recovery. These are the behaviors that shape how you age — the daily practices that move you toward or away from the life you want. But there's another side to aging well, one that's just as important as the habits themselves.

It's the numbers.

Not in a cold or clinical way, but in a clarifying way. Numbers tell the story of what's happening beneath the surface — the trends, the risks, the strengths, and the opportunities. They reveal whether your efforts are working. They show you where to focus. They help you course-correct before small issues become big ones.

Part III is about learning to read your body's dashboard.

Wearable technology is part of that story, but it's only the beginning. Bloodwork, DXA scans, cardiovascular markers, metabolic indicators, and even the numbers from your annual physical all provide signals — signals that can guide your decisions, sharpen your routines, and help you age with intention rather than guesswork.

If Part II was about building the engine, Part III is about installing the gauges.

Now we turn to the data that matters — and how to use it to live longer, stronger, and more aware.

CHAPTER 6 – THE LAW OF MEASUREMENT: WHAT YOU TRACK, YOU IMPROVE

The Law of Measurement is simple: When you know your numbers, you stop guessing.

This next section starts with an apology — and another moment I will never forget.

First, the apology: I am a data nerd. Always have been, always will be.

Second, the moment. It happened almost 40 years ago, and it shaped the way I think about numbers to this day.

A little background. In college, I majored in Industrial Engineering — a perfect fit for me. An IE collects data on systems and uses it to identify and implement improvements. My first job out of school involved capacity and capital planning. I got to recommend how much money a $1B division should spend on equipment. For a young engineer, that was thrilling.

At the time, our market was strong and we needed additional manufacturing equipment. I was tasked with figuring out how many machines of a particular type we needed. Each machine cost $1.4 million — a huge amount of money in the mid-1980s. I labored for days doing the most thorough analysis I knew how to do. When I presented it to my manager, he was pleased. Then came the big moment: presenting to the executive in charge.

I was nervous. This was my first major presentation to someone with real authority. I walked through my analysis and explained that we needed 8.6 machines to meet demand, including all the what-if scenarios I had run. I started to explain the methodology.

The executive almost smiled. He waved his hand dismissively and said he would sign off on 12 machines. "Next presentation, please."

Ouch.

I was disappointed — I didn't even get to explain my logic. But I learned a lesson I've carried ever since: data is important, but interpretation is even more important. I was the gauge. He was the driver. And the driver is the one who makes the decisions.

Such is the case with collecting data for a life well lived. The numbers are informative, but they are just numbers. How we use them — how we interpret them — is what truly matters.

And with that, let's continue our discussion about HRV that we began in the last chapter.

Heart Rate Variability: Understanding Your Body's Daily Signal

If Part III Is About Reading Your Body's Dashboard, HRV Is One of the Most Important Gauges

It's not the only number that matters — far from it — but it's one of the few that gives you a real-time window into how your body is handling stress, recovery, and the demands of daily life.

I've spent years experimenting with HRV. I've tracked it across seasons, training cycles, travel, meditation streaks, red-light therapy, breathwork, and even thyroid fluctuations. I've compared devices, logged thousands of data points, and run my own small-scale experiments.

And what I've learned is this:

HRV is incredibly useful — but only if you understand what it's actually telling you.

Let's break it down.

What HRV Really Measures

This may sound a little redundant — and that's intentional. These terms may not be familiar to many readers, and it's important to understand them before we talk about Heart Rate Variability.

HRV is the variation in time between successive heartbeats, measured in milliseconds. If your heart beats once per second, HRV tells you how much that interval changes from beat to beat — maybe 1.01 seconds between one pair of beats and 0.95 seconds between the next.

That variability is controlled by your autonomic nervous system (ANS), which has two branches:

- Sympathetic ("fight or flight") — mobilizes energy, increases heart rate, prepares you for action
- Parasympathetic ("rest and recover") — slows things down, promotes digestion, healing, and restoration

A higher HRV generally means your parasympathetic system is active and your body is in a state of readiness.

A lower HRV often means stress, fatigue, illness, or overexertion are at play.

HRV isn't about how fast your heart beats — it's about how flexible it is.

A healthy system adapts quickly.

A stressed system becomes rigid.

Why HRV Matters

I first became interested in HRV because I noticed something surprising: on days when my HRV was high, my shooting performance was consistently better. My reaction-ball drills were sharper. My focus was steadier. My coordination felt smoother.

That led me down the rabbit hole.

HRV correlates with:

- reaction time
- emotional regulation
- cognitive performance
- sleep quality
- recovery from training
- resilience to stress
- readiness for physical or mental effort

It's not a magic number, but it's a powerful signal — one that reflects the total load your body is carrying.

What Influences HRV (More Than You Think)

One of the biggest lessons from my experiments is that HRV is influenced by far more than workouts or sleep. It's a whole-system metric, and that means everything counts.

Here are some of the factors I've personally tested:

1. Red Light Therapy

After consistent morning red-light sessions, my HRV increased by roughly 10%. It wasn't a one-day spike — it was a trend. Research supports this: red light can improve mitochondrial efficiency and support recovery.

2. Sleep Environment

A simple eye mask improved my sleep scores and nudged HRV upward. Small changes matter.

3. Overtraining

When I followed my wearable's "readiness" recommendations and pushed hard, my HRV didn't improve — in fact, it dipped. The body doesn't lie.

4. Meditation and Breathwork

Meditation improved my calm scores, but interestingly, my HRV didn't always rise with it. That taught me that HRV reflects physiological stress more than mental calm.

5. Resonance Breathing

Clinically, it's a gold standard for increasing HRV. For me? No measurable effect. A reminder that HRV is personal.

6. Creatine

A supplement I was taking daily. It lowered my HRV. Even though it has the potential to improve strength, cognition, and recovery, I wasn't willing to trade those off for a lowered HRV — so I stopped using it.

7. Thyroid Function

This one was big. When my thyroid levels were off, my HRV dropped. When they normalized, HRV climbed. Medical conditions matter.

8. Seasonality

This surprised me: my HRV was strongly correlated with outside temperature. Higher in the summer, lower in the winter. This pattern has repeated year after year. It makes it challenging to tease out what impacts come from particular interventions versus regular seasonality.

How to Read HRV Like a Scientist, not a Fortune Teller

HRV is powerful, but only if you interpret it correctly. Here's what my year-long experiment taught me:

- Trends matter more than daily numbers. A single low HRV day means nothing. A downward trend over a week means something.
- Nighttime HRV is more reliable than daytime HRV. Daytime HRV is noisy — influenced by movement, stress, caffeine, meetings, and life. Nighttime HRV is cleaner.
- HRV should guide, not dictate. If your wearable says "go hard" but your body says "no," trust your body. If your wearable says "rest" but you feel great, use judgment.
- HRV is one signal, not the whole story. It's a dashboard light — not the engine.
- HRV responds to life load. Deadlines, travel, emotional stress, illness, and even weather all show up in HRV. It's not just about training.

What HRV Can Tell You — and What It Can't

HRV can tell you:

- how well you're recovering
- whether your nervous system is overloaded
- when you might be getting sick
- when to push and when to back off
- how your habits are affecting your physiology

HRV cannot tell you:

- your worth
- your fitness level — it's difficult to compare HRV from person to person
- whether you're "good" or "bad" today

The goal isn't to chase HRV.

The goal is to understand it — and use it as one tool among many to age intentionally.

While I've learned a lot about HRV, there is one resource I've found to be the best summary: Dave Maxfield's book *Up Your HRV*. I recommend it.

But how do we collect HRV data?

Let's look at wearables next.

Wearables: Turning Data into Insight

Fitbit, the first mass-market consumer fitness tracker, launched in 2009. It kicked off what is now a $20-billion market in the United .States. Since then, Apple has emerged as the dominant player with the Apple Watch. Google acquired Fitbit in 2021. Garmin, Samsung, the Oura Ring, and the screen-less Whoop band round out the major players.

So which one do I use?

I started with a Fitbit back in 2015, and today I wear the Fitbit Versa 4. Why? In a word: inertia. After more than a decade of data stored in my Fitbit account, staying put is simply the path of least resistance.

My wife uses an Apple Watch. She chose it because of its fall-detection feature — something that became very important to us. She has a heart condition that can lead to fainting. One day, while I was out on the bike, she fainted, fell down the stairs, and broke her leg. Had she been wearing the Apple Watch then, it would have alerted me immediately.

She's fine now, but that experience changed how we think about technology.

Since then, she has tried to convert me to the Apple Watch. And while I admit that "inertia" might also be code for "laziness," the real reason I haven't switched is that I find Fitbit simpler and easier to use. Fitbit has stayed focused on fitness tracking, while the Apple Watch has become a full-blown mini-computer. All the apps and features feel overwhelming to me. I can navigate the Fitbit app quickly and intuitively.

Recently, Google rolled out an AI-coach update to the Fitbit app. I'm part of the public preview, and so far, I see a lot of potential. I'm eager to see the final release.

How I Use My Fitbit

I wear my Fitbit 24/7 so I can capture sleep data and, most importantly, my overnight HRV. It only comes off when I shower — which is also when it charges. I subscribe to the premium service for additional insights.

Each morning, after I make my way to my dining room office (remember, I don't keep my phone in the bedroom), I check the following:

- Resting heart rate
- Overnight HRV
- Sleep duration and sleep score
- Deep sleep and REM percentages vs. my 30-day average
- Daily readiness score
- Cardio load target and commentary

The readiness score and cardio load target are calculated from the raw data, but I like to look at both the numbers and the interpretation. It takes only a few seconds to take it all in.

Then I correlate the data — and the recommendations — with how I actually feel.

Some days, the commentary is spot-on. For example, today's message reads:

"Your readiness is high, but you've been pushing yourself recently. Low-intensity cardio like cycling and walking can increase blood flow and promote healing."

My cardio load target is 1–73, which means I don't need to be on the couch, but I should take it easy.

Other days, the recommendations don't match my reality at all. I may have done a big bike ride the day before and still be feeling it — but my stats look great and the app suggests I'm ready to climb Mount Everest. On those days, I joke with my wife that Fitbit is trying to kill me again.

That's where veto power comes in. I use the data, the scores, and the recommendations — but I also use my body's signals. Most of the time, the two are aligned. When they're not, I listen to my body. The body truly does keep the score.

A Note on Sleep Data

If you search the internet for "wearable sleep accuracy," you'll find plenty of evidence that these devices aren't as precise as a clinical sleep study. That's true.

But in my experience, the trends are meaningful.

When I started wearing a sleep mask, the difference in my data before and after was obvious. Day to day, I see a strong correlation between how I feel and how much deep and REM sleep I get. When I'm near my 30-day averages, I feel great. When I deviate, I don't feel as sharp.

The absolute numbers matter less to me than how they compare to my own norms.

Why I Watch HRV and Resting Heart Rate

After a year of analyzing my own data, I discovered some patterns that turned out to be extremely useful — especially given my family history.

My father had Graves' disease, an overactive thyroid. My wife had thyroid cancer and had hers removed. So we're a little sensitive to thyroid issues.

A few years ago, I started feeling sluggish. My eyebrows were thinning at the outer edges. My fingernails were brittle. I was often cold. Classic signs of hypothyroidism — the opposite of what my dad experienced.

Bloodwork confirmed a "sub-clinical" hypothyroid condition. My TSH was technically normal, but at the extreme end of the range. And "normal" is a long way from "optimal."

I tried natural approaches and supplements (more on that in the next chapter), and while they helped a little, my doctor and I ultimately decided on a small dose of synthetic thyroid hormone. We now monitor it annually through bloodwork, and my levels are back near the midpoint of the range.

But here's the interesting part:

Between blood draws, my Fitbit gives me early clues.

As my resting heart rate drops, my HRV rises — and vice versa. That's expected: elite athletes have low RHR and high HRV. But in my case, if my RHR drops too low, it means I'm drifting into hypothyroid territory. At one point, my nighttime heart rate was dipping into the high 30s.

On the other hand, if my RHR climbs above my normal range, I'm heading toward hyperthyroid — too much hormone. When that happens, my HRV plummets and my sleep scores tank. They're all tied together.

By watching these trends, I can fine-tune my thyroid dosage — sometimes skipping a day or two when I see the pattern emerging.

I'm not a doctor, and I'm certainly not your doctor. I'm simply sharing how I use my data to guide conversations with my healthcare provider. For me, the results have been clear: I'm no longer cold all the time, my nails look normal, my eyebrows extend all the way out again, and most importantly — I feel great.

Using Fitbit as a Metabolic Dashboard

I don't just look at the Fitbit app first thing in the morning. One of the most powerful tools I use is the calorie-burn data. You may recall from Chapter 3 that I can calculate my daily calorie intake with confidence because my meal plan is standardized and consistent. I don't count calories, weigh food, or track macros. I know what a serving looks like, and I know what each meal contributes to the tank.

When I deviate from the template — which happens occasionally — I don't worry about it. Outliers don't tip the scales, literally or figuratively. But that's only half the equation.

In Chapter 4, we talked about how we burn what we ingest. What I hadn't addressed until now is how to know, with real accuracy, how much we're actually burning — and how to keep the two sides of the equation in sync.

That's where my Fitbit becomes invaluable.

Fitbit tallies all the calories I burn in a day — sleeping, working, watching TV, exercising, even eating — and gives me daily, weekly, monthly, and annual averages.

Last year, I burned an average of 3,150 calories per day. That's not a guess. That's what my Fitbit logged automatically.

I also know that my diet plan produced:

- 2,626 calories on workout days
- 2,284 calories on non-workout days

Since I did intensive cardio five days per week, I can calculate a weighted average of 2,528 calories consumed per day.

It's easy to see how I lost ten pounds over the course of the year. I was burning 3,150 calories and consuming 2,528 — a net deficit.

And yes, I did a little "cheating." If I hadn't, and if you take the rough estimate that a pound of human tissue equals about 3,500 calories, I could have lost 65 pounds based strictly on the math. I blame my wife's angel food cake.

The point is this:

I now have the tools to monitor both inputs and outputs and keep them in balance.

Planning for Reduced Biking Mileage

This data also lets me run "what-if" scenarios. For example, I'm reducing my biking this year from over 10,000 miles to about 6,000. That means fewer calories burned.

I can adjust my fueling plan by reducing my biking fueling calories (fewer cliff bars and stinger waffles) by about 100 calories per day. That means I'll need to burn an average of 2,428 calories per day to avoid weight gain — assuming no cheating.

Fitbit will track that for me. My daily weigh-ins will confirm whether the math is working.

But will I actually hit that target?

Last year, I burned 3,150 calories per day while riding 200 miles per week. If I drop to about 115 miles per week, that's 85 fewer miles. I know that 24 miles of riding equals about 1,000 calories for me. So dropping 85 miles means losing roughly 505 calories per day of burn (spread across the entire week).

That drops my average daily burn from 3,150 to about 2,645 calories.

My margin is now just 217 calories per day — about one handful of peanuts.

I'm going to have to tighten up the snacking.

That's the power of having data and using it with intention. If things go off track, I only need to look at two places:

diet compliance or energy burn.

What About Steps?

You might be wondering about steps. After all, that's the metric most fitness trackers started with. Do I obsess over getting 10,000 steps a day?

Not anymore.

You've probably heard that the 10,000-step goal wasn't based on science. It was created by a Japanese pedometer manufacturer as a marketing tool. It caught on and became urban legend.

When I bought my first Fitbit over a decade ago, I dutifully targeted 10,000 steps a day. And honestly, it wasn't a bad goal — it got me moving.

But I don't track steps anymore because they don't align with my philosophy of moving with intention.

Walking my German shepherd is cardio.

Walking my golden retriever was sniff-time.

Those steps are not the same.

So 10,000 steps may or may not be meaningful depending on what drives them.

A Better Metric: Cardio Load

Fitbit calculates a cardio load score that reflects how hard you're actually pushing your body. I find that far more useful than a simple step count.

Fitbit also gives me a daily goal based on my readiness score. If I agree with the goal, I can track my progress in real time throughout the day.

A Confession — and a Caution

A confession: when I first got my Fitbit, I discovered it would count steps if I just moved my arm. I'm not proud of this, but more than once I sat in my recliner and "walked" without leaving the chair to hit my daily goal.

It didn't improve my fitness. It didn't improve my arm strength. It was silly.

But it taught me something important:

Fitness trackers are tools. They should improve your life, not create anxiety.

Some people get so stressed about their sleep score that they can't sleep. If the data makes your life worse, it's worth asking why you're using the device.

I love data. I love turning data into useful information. But the goal is to use these tools as a positive source of motivation — not a source of stress.

Speaking of Motivation…

Let's look at another type of wearable — the trip computer that sits on the handlebars of my bike.

Bike Computers: Motivation, Measurement, and the Joy of Progress

Bike trip computers have been around a very long time. I still remember the first one I owned several decades ago. The body mounted to the fork of the bike, and every time the wheel made one revolution, a pin attached to a spoke would strike a tiny gear on the device. That gear would rotate just enough to advance a mechanical display showing the distance ridden. It was "stone age" technology compared to today's units — multi-color digital displays with more computing power than what was probably on the NASA space shuttles.

Today, I use a Wahoo Element Bolt. I'd love to tell you I performed an exhaustive evaluation of every unit on the market, but the truth is simpler: it was a gift. Turns out, it was a very good one.

With the addition of three sensors — a chest-mounted heart-rate strap, plus speed and cadence sensors — I can see a wealth of information: moving time, elapsed time, speed, distance, heart rate, pedal cadence, elevation gained, and even which gear I'm in. Add in an app called Strava, and the real magic happens.

Strava is one of the world's leading fitness-tracking platforms, with over 180 million users. It records, analyzes, and shares more than 50 types of activities using GPS data, and it adds a social layer — segment leaderboards, photo sharing, clubs, and community challenges.

Say I'm doing a sprint on my favorite one-mile section of greenway. A quick glance at my computer tells me whether I'm ahead or behind my previous best time — and what my projected finish will be. After the ride, I can compare my performance not only to my own history, but to every athlete who has ridden that same segment that day, that year, or all-time — filtered by age, weight, and sex.

Why does this matter to me? Simple: it keeps me motivated.

Strava tracks my weekly, monthly, and year-to-date progress, so I always know exactly where I stand relative to my goals.

- It shows my fitness level and how it's changing.
- It lets me compete with myself — and with anyone else I choose. That taps into my competitive streak.
- It provides accountability. Friends and family can see my activities, give kudos, and comment.
- It offers challenges that push me to ride on days when my enthusiasm might be flagging. Amazing how a virtual badge can get you out the door.
- After each ride, an AI coach even provides feedback on my effort.

Seeing all this data helps me understand how I'm improving and how my efforts are contributing to my fitness. It gives me that nudge to keep going — both on and off the bike. It also keeps me connected to other athletes. My wife has two cousins in Poland who are professional-level cyclists. I see their daily activities, and I'm motivated by what they do. On a vacation visit,

I even had the chance to ride with them. Now, when I see them ride those same routes on Strava, it brings a smile to my face. I've been there — not just virtually, but in the real world.

Let's turn our attention to another metric I use to understand how my body is performing and adapting.

Next up: VO_2 Max.

VO_2 Max: The Strongest Predictor of Longevity I've Ever Measured

If you've ever done a VO_2 max test, it's an experience you don't forget. Let me paint a picture. You exercise at increasing levels of difficulty — on a treadmill or a bike — while wearing a mask connected to a machine that measures how much oxygen you inhale and how much carbon dioxide you exhale. In my case, the technician kept me running around 6 MPH while steadily increasing the incline of the treadmill, all while encouraging me to keep pushing until my body simply couldn't use oxygen at a higher rate. Those ten minutes felt a lot longer. I get a little claustrophobic wearing the mask, so it's not something I look forward to. But the data is invaluable.

VO_2 max is your body's maximum oxygen consumption during intense exercise. In plain English, it tells you how efficiently your body can use oxygen — a direct reflection of your cardiovascular fitness. A higher VO_2 max means better endurance, faster recovery, and greater overall physical capacity.

It's also one of the strongest predictors of longevity ever studied.

Why VO_2 Max Matters for Aging Well

Decades of research have shown that cardiorespiratory fitness — measured by VO_2 max — is tightly linked to how long and how well we live.

Here are the highlights from the scientific literature:

- Higher fitness = lower mortality. A landmark study of over 10,000 adults found that each 1-MET increase in fitness was associated with a 13% reduction in all-cause mortality (Blair et al., JAMA, 1989).
- VO_2 max predicts survival better than traditional risk factors. A meta-analysis of 33 studies showed that individuals with high cardiorespiratory fitness had a 47% lower risk of death than those with low fitness (Kodama et al., JAMA, 2009).
- Elite fitness dramatically reduces risk. In a study of 122,000 patients, those with "elite" fitness levels had an 80% lower mortality risk compared to low-fitness individuals (Mandsager et al., JAMA Network Open, 2018).
- VO_2 max declines with age — unless you train. Research shows VO_2 max typically drops 5–10% per decade after age 30, but endurance training can cut that decline in half or even reverse it (Fitzgerald et al., Journal of Applied Physiology, 1997).

In other words:

VO_2 max is not just a fitness metric — it's a longevity metric.

My VO_2 Max Results — and What They Mean

I had my first VO_2 max test done in August 2023 to establish a baseline. I skipped 2024 and repeated the test in 2025. My 2023 score was 43.2 — already high for my age. I wasn't sure what to expect in 2025. VO_2 max usually declines with age, and I was hoping just to hold steady.

Instead, I was pleasantly surprised:

my VO_2 max increased by 9.7%, rising to 47.4 — in the "superior" range for my age group.

The cardio work is paying off.

How I Train to Improve VO_2 Max

Improving VO_2 max comes down to two key training approaches:

1. Zone 2 Training (Steady, Moderate Effort)

This is the foundation. For me, that means long sessions of moderate-effort cycling — my average ride is a bit over 40 miles at around 16 mph. Zone 2 builds mitochondrial density, improves fat oxidation, and increases the body's ability to use oxygen efficiently.

2. High-Intensity Interval Training (HIIT)

This is the accelerator — short bursts of high effort followed by recovery. We discussed this in Chapter 4, but it's worth repeating.

At the gym, I finish each strength session with 10 minutes of treadmill time — either walking uphill or doing intervals of short sprints followed by walking. I also incorporate HIIT segments into my bike rides. I target at least one treadmill HIIT session each week.

The science backs this up:

HIIT improves VO_2 max twice as much as steady-state training (Wisløff et al., Circulation, 2007).

Together, Zone 2 and HIIT form a powerful combination — one that not only boosts performance but also supports long-term health and longevity.

Why VO_2 Max Belongs in Your Dashboard

If Part III is about learning to read your body's gauges, VO_2 max is one of the most important ones. It tells you:

- how strong your cardiovascular system is
- how well your body uses oxygen
- how resilient you are to physical stress
- how your fitness is trending over time
- how your training is affecting your long-term health

And unlike many metrics, VO_2 max is highly trainable. You can improve it at any age.

For me, the increase from 43.2 to 47.4 wasn't just a number — it was confirmation that the work I'm doing is moving me toward the life I want to live. Stronger. More capable. More resilient.

And, if the research is right, likely to live longer — and better — too.

Should you subject yourself to the test? Absolutely. I see the $200 or so that I spent as a solid investment in my long-term aging program. Some wearables do provide an estimate of VO_2 max, but their accuracy can be questionable — my own wearable consistently overestimates mine. Even with my aversion to wearing the mask, I've found the formal test worthwhile, and I plan to repeat it periodically to track my progress with precision. If you absolutely can't tolerate the test, then at least pay attention to the trends your wearable shows you — even if the absolute numbers aren't perfect, the direction of change still tells a meaningful story.

And here's a tip: reducing body fat while maintaining lean tissue through smart nutrition, strength training, and cardio is one of the most effective ways to improve VO_2 max. But how do you know whether you're actually achieving positive body re-composition? Read on. A DEXA scan will tell us everything we need to know.

DEXA: The Gold Standard for Understanding Your Body Composition

If VO_2 max tells you how well your engine is performing, a DEXA scan tells you what the engine is made of. It's one of the most precise tools we have for understanding body composition — not just weight, but the quality of that weight. And when it comes to aging well, that distinction matters.

A DEXA scan (Dual-Energy X-ray Absorptiometry) uses two low-dose X-ray beams to measure bone density, fat mass, and lean mass with remarkable accuracy. It's painless, quick, and far more informative than a scale or a tape measure. For anyone serious about aging intentionally, it's one of the most valuable data points you can collect.

I had my first DEXA scan done in August 2023. I wanted a baseline — a clear picture of where I stood before making changes to my training and nutrition. The scan gave me exactly that: a detailed breakdown of my body fat percentage, visceral fat, bone density, and lean mass distribution. It was the first time I truly understood what was happening inside my body, not just what the mirror or scale showed.

I repeated the scan in 2024 and again in 2025. That three-year sequence gave me something even more valuable than a snapshot — it gave me a trend line. And the trend was encouraging. My body fat percentage dropped to 15.5%. My visceral fat — the dangerous kind that wraps around organs — decreased. My lean mass actually increased. In other words, I wasn't just losing weight; I was improving the composition of that weight. That's the holy grail of aging well.

Why does this matter? Because body re-composition — losing fat while maintaining or gaining lean mass — is one of the most powerful levers we have for improving health-span. Lower visceral fat is associated with reduced cardiovascular risk, better metabolic health, and improved longevity. Higher lean mass supports mobility, strength, balance, and independence as we age.

And here's where the DEXA scan becomes essential:

you can't manage what you can't measure.

A scale can't tell you whether you lost fat or muscle. A tape measure can't tell you whether your visceral fat is creeping up. The DEXA scan cuts through all of that and gives you the truth. In my case, over the last year, I had lost 10 pounds — but DEXA revealed that I had actually lost 14 pounds of fat while gaining 4 pounds of lean mass. I could see the difference on the report: a heat-map image comparing my last two scans, color-coded for lean versus fat tissue. Not only were there fewer areas lighting up as fat, but my entire body profile looked leaner. My visceral fat had dropped to almost nothing. Very motivating indeed.

For me, the scans validated that my training and nutrition were working. They also highlighted areas to improve. My legs and glutes were still showing less lean mass than I would like — something I wouldn't have known without the scan. That insight allowed me to adjust my strength training to address the imbalance (biking tends to work the quadriceps hard, but not the hamstrings and glutes). Note that it is virtually impossible to spot reduce fat mass – but lean mass can be added selectively through targeted strength training of specific areas combined with adequate protein intake and recovery.

The DEXA scan also ties directly into VO_2 max. Reducing body fat while maintaining lean mass is one of the most effective ways to improve VO_2 max — because your body becomes more efficient at moving itself through space. But without a DEXA scan, you're guessing whether you're actually achieving positive body re-composition.

Should you get a DEXA scan?

If you're serious about aging well, I believe the answer is yes. It's a small investment for a wealth of information. I plan to continue repeating mine periodically to track trends over time — not obsessively, but intentionally. Once a year is a good cadence for me. In between scans, I can get a sense of how my composition is trending based on how my clothes and wedding ring fit. In fact, I had to get a new wedding band because my ring finger is now a size smaller.

The scan gives you a baseline. It gives you direction. And it gives you confidence that the work you're doing is moving you toward the life you want to live.

How do you find a source for the scan? I simply did an internet search for "DEXA scan near me". Several local options were available. For consistency, I have used the same facility, the same machine and the same technician for every scan. He takes the time to make sure I understand every single bit of data / information on the resulting report – especially the changes from scan to scan. Invaluable.

The Magic Number 5

So, as important as VO_2 max and body-fat percentage are to me, there is one number that may trump them both.

Five.

I bet you're tingling with anticipation, because you've probably never seen this "secret hack" to aging well in any other book. Don't let me keep you in suspense. The number 5 represents the sum of the most important appointments I schedule every single year:

1. My annual physical with my primary care doctor
2. My annual skin check with my dermatologist
3. My annual routine eye exam with my optometrist
4. My semi-annual dental cleaning and check-up
5. …and the second semi-annual dental cleaning and check-up

These visits generate a tremendous amount of measurable data — which is why they belong in this chapter. But this is also where I step onto my soapbox for a moment.

First, I'm a guy, so my magic number is 5. For the women reading this, your number is going to be a little higher — and I want to address that right away. You need to add your regular OB/GYN visits and your mammograms. This last one carries personal weight for me: my wife just had her first clean mammogram after a year of fighting breast cancer. Early detection — through routine screening — made all the difference. Surgery and radiation were successful because the cancer was caught early.

Please don't fall into the "it won't happen to me" trap. Early detection dramatically improves outcomes.

And since we're talking about the big "C," let's address another screening that doesn't happen annually but is just as important: the colonoscopy. I get mine every five years. Yes, the prep is unpleasant. But it's a whole lot more pleasant than colon cancer. If these appointments aren't already on your calendar, pause this book and schedule them.

My Rules for Doctoring

1. Find healthcare professionals you like — and stick with them.

I've talked before about balancing high-tech with high-touch. This is another example. Digital medical records are great, but nothing replaces a doctor who knows you, your history, and your life. Three of my four doctors have been with me for years. I'm currently "training" a new dentist — he bought the practice from the dentist I'd seen for decades. He's coming along nicely.

2. Don't lie to your doctors.

Yes, the forms can be embarrassing. But if you're using recreational drugs, tell them. If you drink alcohol, tell them — and how much. If you're a nudist who hates sunscreen, tell them. If you're struggling with mental health, tell them. Don't minimize symptoms. Don't tell them what you think they want to hear. Don't commit lies of omission.

My mom lived to 86, but she was notorious for telling her doctors fictional stories. Luckily, I was there to gently correct things with a wink, a nod, or a follow-up email. Please don't do this. Your doctors can only help you if you give them the truth.

Let's Get into the Details — Starting with the Dentist

Numerous studies show that routine dental care doesn't just protect your teeth — it protects your life. A 2024 review in The Lancet Healthy Longevity found that poor oral health is linked to cardiovascular disease, diabetes, Alzheimer's disease, rheumatoid arthritis, pneumonia, and even certain cancers. A massive national study in Japan showed that older adults with better oral health lived significantly longer than those with poor dental status. And a 2024 systematic review in BDJ Open confirmed that people who maintain regular dental visits have far better oral-health outcomes over time.

In other words: brushing, flossing, and showing up twice a year isn't vanity — it's longevity.

I still come home after every dentist visit and proudly tell my wife, "Hey — no cavities!" That streak ended this year. I'd been having cold sensitivity in a molar, and the dentist found a crack that required a crown. While preparing the tooth, he discovered a hidden cavity in the adjacent tooth that didn't show up on X-ray. I walked out with a two-fer — and no more cold sensitivity.

I attribute my long run of good dental health to regular checkups and good hygiene at home, including flossing. And here comes another confession. Remember my story about swinging my arm in the recliner to inflate my step count? I used to do something similar with flossing. The week before my cleaning, I'd break out the floss and try to undo 5.75 months of neglect. Did it work? Not really. The hygienist always knew.

One year, I finally committed to daily flossing. Guess what? The hygienist could tell — and the cleaning took far less time. Less time with sharp metal tools in my mouth is a win.

If that isn't enough to convince you, the studies above should do the trick.

I'm trying to keep my teeth in good condition for as long as I can. I like to smile and eat without pain. I imagine you do too.

Eyes: The Windows to Your Future

My eye doctor is also a family friend — we grew up together. I've had annual eye exams since I was six years old. I still remember getting my first pair of glasses. I had no idea the world looked like that.

My commitment to annual exams intensified about ten years ago when my mom was diagnosed with wet age-related macular degeneration (AMD). Like my wife's breast cancer, it was caught early during a routine visit. She received a series of eye injections, and by her mid-80s she only needed to see the retinologist once a year. Early detection and consistent care saved her vision. Untreated, AMD can lead to blindness.

Our eyes are essential to our functioning — but they're not the largest organ we have. That honor belongs to our skin.

Skin: Your Largest Organ, and One Worth Protecting

Who enjoys sitting half-naked in a cold exam room with a paper towel over your lap while a dermatologist examines every inch of your skin under a bright magnifier? Not me. But I go every year.

Why? Because I love being outdoors. Even with sunscreen, I still get sun damage — I inherited fair Finnish skin from my mom's side of the family. My dermatologist knows me well. She knows I cycle. She knows I'm outside a lot. She was the one who suggested wearing a beanie under my helmet to block UV rays coming through the vent holes.

Even with precautions, I still need topical chemotherapy treatment every 2–3 years for sun-damaged skin — especially on my face and, this year, the top of my head. The cream is remarkable: it targets damaged cells while leaving healthy skin intact. But for two weeks, I look like a leper, and I have to stay out of the sun. No outdoor biking.

Still, that's far better than malignant skin cancer. With early detection, the survival rate is 99%. That's enough to keep me going back to that cold room and bright light.

And Now, the Appointment With the Most Measurable Results: The Annual Physical

Get out your stethoscope — this is where the numbers really start to matter.

The Annual Physical: Your Most Data-Rich Appointment of the Year

Preparation for my annual physical starts about three weeks before my appointment. That's when I go to the lab for my blood draw.

Confession time again… I used to schedule my physical in early December and get my blood drawn before Thanksgiving. That way I could go all-in on turkey day dinner (and the days of leftovers that follow) without worrying about how it would affect my labs. And again — that was silly. These days, I'm far less focused on gorging myself at meals and far more focused on maintaining good health all the time. It's a better way to live.

My doctor — who I've seen for decades — is my age. He can relate to the things we're both experiencing. He has always had me get my labs done well before my appointment so we actually have data to discuss. That's very different from my wife's annual physical, where her blood draw happens at the end of the visit. I prefer my doctor's approach, and if he didn't do it that way, I'd ask him to — or find someone who would.

This is where the balance of high-touch and high-tech really matters. I value the relationship I have with my doctor, but I also love having all my lab results available online — often before he even sees them. But having early access to results can be a double-edged sword. Numbers often require interpretation. Seeing them ahead of time lets me look at trends and prepare questions, but even with all the tools available today, including AI, I still rely on my doctor's expertise to help me understand what the numbers mean. I always walk away from my appointment a more knowledgeable patient.

Five Ways to Be an Informed, Prepared Patient

These five principles keep me grounded, organized, and ready to make the most of my annual physical — and they tie directly back to the data I collect from my wearables and daily habits.

1. Bring your trends, not just your questions.

Doctors see snapshots. You see the movie.

Your wearable gives you:

- resting heart rate trends
- sleep trends
- activity trends
- weight trends
- blood pressure readings (if you track at home)

Your doctor doesn't automatically have access to any of that. Bringing trends — not isolated numbers — gives context that makes your appointment far more productive.

2. Create a one-page health summary.

This isn't medical advice — it's organization.

A simple sheet with:

- medications and supplements
- recent symptoms or changes
- questions you want answered
- any relevant data trends

Doctors love this. It respects their time and ensures you don't forget something important.

3. Don't save your questions for the last minute.

People often freeze up in the exam room.

Preparing questions in advance:

- reduces anxiety
- keeps the conversation focused
- ensures you get the answers you came for

This is your time — use it intentionally.

4. Remember: your doctor is a partner, not a judge.

Shame, embarrassment, and half-truths get in the way of good care.

Your doctor isn't grading you. They're trying to help.

Honesty — even when it's uncomfortable — is one of the most powerful tools you have.

5. Don't let the internet scare you.

Seeing your lab results early can trigger doom-scrolling.

Use the internet to:

- understand terminology
- prepare questions
- learn about trends

But let your doctor interpret the results. That's their job.

What My Doctor Checks Each Year

Before the appointment, my doctor orders a standard set of blood tests. These typically include:

- ALT – a marker related to liver health
- Basic Metabolic Panel (BMP) – information about kidney function, electrolytes, and blood sugar. (Some doctors order a Comprehensive Metabolic Panel instead, depending on context and insurance rules.)
- Lipid Panel – cholesterol and triglycerides
- TSH – a thyroid marker -He didn't used to run this until I told him about my sluggish-thyroid symptoms. It pays to have open conversations with your doctor.

A Missing but Essential Number: PSA

There's one more blood-work item my doctor checks each year that deserves its own mention: PSA, a marker related to prostate health. Guys — this one is as important to us as mammograms are to the women in our lives. It's a simple test, it's part of the standard blood panel for many men our age, and it gives you and your doctor valuable information to track over time. I get mine done every year.

Once I'm called back from the waiting room, height and weight are checked so BMI can be calculated. A savvy reader of this book will already know their BMI from the formula in Chapter 3. Blood pressure is measured next. I check mine at home occasionally, so there shouldn't be any surprises.

My doctor performs a physical exam, and then we talk. This is my time to make sure he knows about any changes in my life and to get my questions answered. It's also when we make plans for the future. For example, I had read that a large portion of U.S. adults have suboptimal vitamin D levels. I didn't think I was one of them, but I wanted a baseline so I'd have a reference point going forward. He ordered the test.

Why This Matters for Aging Well

Knowing our numbers — and understanding them — is a powerful part of aging intentionally. Having real conversations with our medical team helps us make informed decisions. Being your own advocate is key. Just like with weight, we don't want to keep our heads in the sand.

Knowledge is power. And when you combine that knowledge with trusted professionals who can help you interpret the data, you give yourself the best chance to live your best life for as long as you live.

Chapter 6 Summary: Your Body's Dashboard

- You can't manage what you don't measure.
- Wearables give you real-time insight into how your body performs and recovers.
- HRV helps you understand stress, readiness, and recovery.
- Fitbit and other trackers show your true energy burn — not guesses.
- Consistent routines make calorie intake predictable and sustainable.
- Cardio load matters more than step counts; move with intention.

- Bike computers turn effort into data and data into motivation.
- VO_2 max is one of the strongest predictors of longevity.
- You can improve VO_2 max at any age with Zone 2 and HIIT.
- DEXA reveals what the scale can't — fat, muscle, bone, and visceral fat.
- Body recomposition is the real goal: less fat, stable or rising lean mass.
- Trends matter more than snapshots — your wearables hold the long view.
- Your "Magic Number 5" appointments keep you ahead of problems.
- Early detection saves lives — don't skip your screenings.
- Bring your data to your doctor; they don't see what your wearable sees.
- Prepare questions, bring trends, and treat your doctor as a partner.
- Knowledge + action = intentional aging.

Your Turn

You've now seen how powerful it can be to measure what matters. This is where you shift from reading to doing. Your job isn't to track everything — it's to pick one or two meaningful signals and start experimenting.

Here are a few simple ways to begin:

1. Use your wearable — or consider getting one

If you already have a wearable, start paying attention to the trends that matter most to you. If you don't have one, this is a great moment to consider it. Even the simplest devices can give you:

- Resting heart rate
- HRV
- Sleep patterns
- Activity levels
- Cardio load or readiness

You don't need perfect accuracy — you just need consistent trends.

2. Choose one experiment to run for the next two weeks

Pick something you're curious about:

- HRV and recovery
- A new exercise routine
- A dietary tweak
- Red light therapy
- Morning sunlight
- Evening wind-down habits

Run the experiment. Watch the trend. Adjust.

This is how you build your own personal "owner's manual."

3. Make your "Five Appointments" — and prepare for them

If you haven't already, schedule the five appointments that anchor your health year:

- Annual physical
- Eye exam
- Dental exams
- Skin check

And when the time comes, bring your data.

Your doctor sees a snapshot.

You see the movie.

4. Consider more advanced tools if they fit your goals

If you're active, endurance-oriented, or simply curious, you might explore:

- A bike computer
- A running watch with advanced metrics
- A chest-strap HR monitor for more precise data

These aren't required — but they can deepen your understanding of how your body responds to training.

5. Look into local options for DEXA and VO_2 Max testing

These two tests give you a clear, objective picture of:

- Body composition
- Bone density
- Metabolic health

- Aerobic capacity

Search for local sports performance labs, university exercise physiology departments, or medical imaging centers. Many offer these tests at reasonable prices.

6. Keep it simple, keep it playful

You're learning how your body responds to the choices you make.

Pick one thing. Measure it. Experiment. Adjust. Repeat.

This is how you build a life that ages well — one small, intentional step at a time.

The Law of Measurement is simple: When you know your numbers, you stop guessing.

When you stop guessing, you start improving.

And when you start improving — even in small, steady ways — you change the trajectory of your aging.

➤ IT'S NOT WHAT YOU KNOW, IT'S WHAT YOU DO. ➤

By now, you've built a dashboard for your life. You know how to track your energy, your movement, your composition, and your health. You've learned how to gather the right data and how to partner with your medical team. That's the Law of Measurement — the foundation of intentional aging.

But knowing your numbers is only half the story. The real breakthroughs happen when you start asking a different kind of question:

"What happens if I change this?"

That's where we're headed next.

Chapter 7 is about embracing the mindset that your body is a laboratory — a place where you can run small, safe, intentional experiments to discover what helps you feel better, move better, and age better. It's where curiosity becomes a tool, feedback becomes fuel, and your daily life becomes a series of learnable, repeatable tests.

Let's step into the lab.

CHAPTER 7 — THE LAW OF EXPERIMENTATION: TRY, TEST, ITERATE

The Law of Experimentation is simple: When you treat your body like a laboratory, you stop fearing change.

"You think we've gotten more curious since entering our 60s?" That was the question my wife and I tossed around after dinner the other night. Our consensus: yes, we have. And because curiosity is now our default setting, the next step was obvious — we asked AI.

AI isn't perfect, but the relevance and reliability of the answers seem to improve every day. So what did our friendly assistant tell us? It turns out there is a general tendency to become more curious as we age. Why? It may have something to do with competence (ring a bell from Chapter 2?), lower anxiety, and having a little more time and mental bandwidth.

As we age, we get better at the things we do. We're more competent in our jobs, in managing our homes, in our relationships. The kids are out on their own. We have fewer money worries. Life feels a little less chaotic. And when the noise quiets down, curiosity has room to grow.

That extra curiosity can put more golden moments into our golden years. In that spirit — and in the hope that my experiences might spark some curiosity of your own — let's walk through a few of the experiments that have taken place in my "lab."

The HRV Deep Dive: My Most Ambitious Experiment

The single most ambitious study I've undertaken in recent years was my year-long rabbit-hole dive into HRV. It was also one of the most beneficial. Once I learned what HRV was, I wanted to know how to improve it — and how to use it as a tool for living better.

So I entered full engineer mode. I collected data on everything I could measure and calculated correlation coefficients that would have made my statistics professors proud. I tracked:

- readiness score
- daytime HRV
- nighttime HRV
- sleep score
- stress score
- cardio zone minutes
- resting heart rate
- meditation score
- even the daily high temperature

I read books, research articles, and anything else I could get my hands on. For a data nerd like me, it was fun.

I even correlated HRV with eye-hand coordination using reaction balls — tennis-sized balls with ten flat spots that make them bounce unpredictably. Every morning, I'd go to the garage, grab two balls, and alternate bouncing and catching them with both hands counting the number of successful catches in 60 seconds. Only after the trial would I check my HRV score so I wouldn't bias the results. The correlations were fascinating — and the cardio from chasing runaway balls wasn't bad either.

It was a lot. But it led to real, lasting changes that improved my health and my life.

I improved my sleep hygiene

- darker room
- eye mask
- refined sleep schedule
- cooler temperature
- no food or drink three hours before bed

I started wearing blue-blocking glasses at night

I adjusted a few supplements (more on that soon)

The Earthing Experiment

Another experiment was testing whether short-term "earthing" could influence HRV. I went outside, took multiple daytime HRV readings to get a stable baseline, then removed my shoes and socks and stood on the bare ground. I repeated the process several times.

The result? No measurable difference.

But curiosity doesn't stop at one test. I bought a grounding mat to see if there might be long-term effects. I still don't know definitively, but it certainly isn't hurting anything — and as I've mentioned earlier, my resistance to viruses has been unusually strong these last few years. Coincidence? Maybe. But the experiment continues.

Not Every Experiment Needs a Spreadsheet

Not all experiments need to be as data-heavy as the HRV project. Small things add up. And while I love quantitative analysis, qualitative analysis — simply noticing how something makes you feel — works too.

Sometimes the inspiration comes from solving a problem.

I've had tendonitis from time to time, as many people who lift weights eventually do. Tendonitis is often managed with rest, ice, compression, elevation, and over-the-counter pain relievers. I'm good with ice, but I wanted something more. After some online sleuthing, I found two products:

- Handmaster Plus, a hand exerciser
- Tendon Trak, a strap that helps reduce tendon irritation

Both made a noticeable difference. The only downside was when someone saw the strap around my ankle and asked if I was on house arrest. I didn't care — I was walking without pain.

Another example: my pillow was overdue for replacement. I found one with customizable inner layers. I tried a few configurations and settled on the one that felt best. I didn't track sleep data for each version — I just paid attention. And the improvement in sleep quality was real.

My general rule: if something has decent reviews, isn't expensive, and poses little risk, I'll try it. Curiosity plus low downside equals a worthwhile experiment.

Diet as an Ongoing Experiment

The diet I presented in Chapter 3 didn't appear out of thin air. It evolved through years of trial, error, and thoughtful research. Three criteria guided me:

1. Fuel for performance and longevity
2. Reduce migraine attacks
3. Keep it simple to plan, prepare, and eat

Protein was a major focus — I wanted enough to build muscle even while reducing body fat. My diet delivers that, roughly one gram per pound of body weight.

The diet also provides the fuel I need for the levels of cardio I choose to do. This isn't left to chance – it is designed for success so that my exercise sessions are fruitful.

Migraine prevention, however, has been a lifelong challenge. Triggers are inconsistent and unpredictable. Caffeine might cause an attack today but not tomorrow. Sugar might be fine one day and a disaster the next. It takes patience and curiosity to identify patterns.

Over time, I've learned I'm sensitive to:

- caffeine (including chocolate — sad face)
- large doses of sugar
- vasodilators like beets
- MSG
- tyramine-rich foods
- smoked or cured meats
- aged cheeses
- fermented foods
- overripe fruits

It has taken more than 50 years to understand these triggers — and it's still a work in progress.

Keeping my diet simple and consistent helps me avoid triggers. Eating most meals at home gives me control over ingredients. The meals are easy to prepare, flexible, satisfying, and predictable. I don't have to calculate macros every day — I know what I'm getting.

And yes, my wife and I still have "discussions" about serving sizes. When in doubt, we bring out the scale. I'm usually wrong. But we both have a good visual sense of portions now — no measuring required.

If your diet isn't as consistent as mine, you can still develop rules of thumb and use apps to do the calculations for you.

Supplements: Experiments From My Lab (my body)

Let me come right out and say it: I am very picky about what I put into my body. Call me risk-averse and intentional. A lot of people are searching for the silver-bullet pill, powder, or injectable that will shortcut the hard work of maintaining a healthy body and brain. That's not me.

I'd rather be intentional about what I eat, how I move, and how I recover—day after day, year after year. With that mindset, I'm not easily convinced to ingest whatever shows up in my news feed as the latest longevity miracle.

What follows are simply experiments from my lab (my body). I'm not a doctor. What has worked (or not worked) for me may not be right for you. Please work with your healthcare provider when it comes to supplements.

Part 1 – Supplements That Made the Cut

Magnesium citrate

Several studies suggest that magnesium supplementation can reduce the frequency and severity of migraines, especially in people who are deficient. As a lifelong migraine sufferer, that caught my attention.

The side effects are usually mild—soft stools being the main one. I already get magnesium from my diet, but I started by taking 250 mg in the evening about an hour before bed. A nice side benefit was muscle relaxation and better sleep. Because migraine is so complex, I can't honestly quantify the exact reduction in attacks, but even if a few are prevented each year, that's a win for me.

To reduce the GI side effects, I dropped to 125 mg per night. That seems to be my sweet spot. Magnesium citrate has earned a permanent place in my lineup.

Fish oil

Fish oil, rich in omega-3 fatty acids (EPA and DHA), has been associated with benefits for heart, brain, joint, and eye health in many studies. It may help lower triglycerides, support blood pressure management, and reduce inflammation. Potential downsides include increased bleeding risk, possible blood-pressure effects, and immune modulation—especially at higher doses or in combination with certain medications.

Given my active lifestyle, fish oil feels like a good fit. I mix it into my smoothie on days when I'm not working out immediately afterward (my workout smoothie is a low-fat version to keep digestion light before exercise). Because of concerns about mercury and rancidity, I only use third-party-tested products. This is definitely one to discuss with your medical provider if you're on other medications or have health conditions.

Beet root powder

I came across a study showing that beetroot juice—thanks to its nitrate content—can improve cycling performance and endurance. Juicing beets, however, is a messy ordeal. A little research led me to beetroot powders like SuperBeets, which make it easy to mix a serving into water.

Beets boost nitric oxide production in the body (not to be confused with nitrous oxide, the "laughing gas" at the dentist).

Nitric oxide is a vasodilator, which is a mixed blessing for me because vasodilation can trigger migraines. I've been using beetroot powder for several years now, usually with breakfast. Nitric oxide test strips show improved levels, and I feel a difference on longer rides—especially if I forget to take it.

So far, my migraine concerns haven't materialized, but as I continue to reduce my migraine frequency, beetroot may be something I need to revisit. For now, it stays in the lineup.

Electrolyte mix

On hot cycling days, I add an electrolyte mix to my water bottle to replace what I lose in sweat. The one I use has modest sodium and chloride, plus vitamin C, potassium, phosphorus, magnesium, zinc, and manganese. On very long rides (50+ miles), I'll sometimes take a bit of extra potassium afterward to help stave off cramping.

A fun contrast: when I was biking in Poland, the pros there simply mixed a little honey in their water bottles. They generally don't ride in the same heat I do at home. (Side note: beets are a staple there too—morning beetroot shots are common.)

That's it. That's all I currently allow past my lips in the supplement category.

Part 2 – Supplements That Didn't Make the Cut

Daily multivitamin

Decades ago, I tried several multivitamins. Most of them upset my stomach, so I eventually settled on a chewable children's vitamin as "insurance" for my not-so-great diet. I took those for years.

Once I cleaned up my diet, I stopped. I no longer saw the need. More recent research has reported that in large groups of generally healthy adults, daily multivitamins don't appear to reduce overall mortality. Some newer work suggests there may be potential cognitive benefits in certain older adults with cardiovascular disease, but the picture is still evolving.

For now, I'm comfortable skipping a daily multivitamin and focusing on getting the nutrition I need from food. The only obvious change I've noticed is less colorful urine.

Rhodiola extract

Rhodiola was one I was a little excited about. Some evidence suggests it may help with stress, mood, and possibly HRV. It can also interact with medications and certain conditions, so it's one to discuss with a doctor.

I didn't have any of the major risk factors, so I tried it. What did I notice? Honestly, not much. I couldn't tell any meaningful difference, so this one didn't make the cut.

Pregnenolone

Pregnenolone is a steroid hormone precursor—the starting point for many hormones in the body, including thyroid hormones. It's synthesized from cholesterol. In theory, supplementing it might help support hormone production.

When I tried it, I initially felt great. I thought my thyroid issues were solved. But my blood test results were erratic. One concern with supplements in general is variability in dose from batch to batch or even pill to pill.

I can't say for sure that's what happened, but I can say that when I stopped pregnenolone and switched to a prescription thyroid medication, my levels stabilized. I'm not sorry I experimented, but for me, it didn't provide the consistent effect I was hoping for. This is a potent supplement—definitely one I'd only consider again under close medical supervision.

Brazil nuts

Brazil nuts aren't a supplement, but I was using them like one. They're extremely rich in selenium, a mineral important for thyroid function. No surprise why I was interested.

The problem is that a single Brazil nut can contain more than the full daily requirement of selenium. A handful can push you into toxicity territory, with symptoms like hair loss and GI distress. When I looked at my diet, I realized I was already getting plenty of selenium from food. Brazil nuts were out.

Creatine

This one won't win me many points with my gym buddies. Creatine is one of the most studied and widely used supplements in the fitness world. It's well-known for increasing muscle size and strength, and there's emerging research suggesting possible brain benefits as well. The body makes about 1 gram per day; typical supplemental doses are 3–5 grams daily after an optional loading phase.

Since it's generally regarded as safe for most healthy people, I decided to try it. I felt like a beast in the gym, and after a few weeks, I could see a difference.

So why did I stop?

This experiment overlapped with my HRV study—and my HRV crashed. Not just a bad day or two; the whole distribution shifted downward and stayed there. I haven't found much in the literature to explain this, but for me, it was real. I also felt a bit bloated and, if I'm honest, like I was "cheating" by artificially inflating my muscles.

I want to build muscle, but not at the expense of my HRV. Creatine was out.

Protein powder

This is another one that may not endear me to my workout friends. You might have noticed there's no protein powder in my smoothie recipe. It used to be there.

My diet already provides about 1 gram of protein per pound of body weight—plenty to support muscle maintenance and growth. But during rides after my protein-boosted smoothie, I started having serious stomach issues. Not mild discomfort—"I'm not sure I'm going to make it home" kind of upset.

So I put my lab coat on.

I suspected something in the smoothie. I didn't want it to be the protein powder. I removed or swapped ingredients one by one:

- blueberries
- fish oil (this was before my low-fat performance version)
- chia seeds
- yogurt
- milk

No change. The last step was removing the protein powder.

Riding nirvana.

Maybe it was a bad batch, so I tried another brand. Same problem. As it turns out, one of the first signs of too much protein can be GI distress. I was living that reality.

Out went the protein powder. For me, it was simply too much of a good thing.

This is how I approach supplements: with curiosity, caution, and a willingness to run experiments—but also a willingness to stop when the data (or my body) says, "enough."

When you treat your body as a laboratory, even your supplement shelf becomes a place for thoughtful testing, not blind faith.

Chapter 7 Summary: The Law of Experimentation

- Curiosity grows with age when competence rises and anxiety falls. More mental bandwidth creates space for exploration and self-discovery.

- Your body is a laboratory, not a mystery. Small, safe experiments reveal what truly works for you.
- HRV is a powerful feedback tool for testing lifestyle changes.
- Data-driven experiments uncover patterns you can't see day-to-day.
- Sleep hygiene improvements often produce measurable gains.
- Blue-light reduction can support better nighttime recovery.
- Not every experiment needs numbers; how you feel matters too.
- Problem-solving sparks experimentation—pain, discomfort, or frustration can be catalysts.
- Simple tools (reaction balls, pillows, straps, mats) can produce meaningful insights.
- Diet is an ongoing experiment shaped by performance, health, and triggers.
- Identifying migraine triggers requires patience, curiosity, and consistency.
- Keeping meals simple reduces guesswork and improves control.
- Supplements belong in the lab too—test, observe, adjust, or discard.
- What works for others may not work for you; personalization is the point.

- Curiosity + feedback = better choices, better habits, better aging.

Your Turn

Use this chapter to build your own mindset of experimentation. You don't need a lab coat, spreadsheets, or fancy equipment. You just need curiosity, consistency, and the willingness to learn from your own life.

- Pick one area of your life to experiment with. Sleep, nutrition, movement, recovery, stress, or daily routines — choose one. Define a simple question. What happens if I change this?" is enough. Keep it small and specific. Run a 7-day test. Adjust one variable. Don't overhaul your life. Change one thing and observe.
- Track something — anything. HRV, sleep score, mood, energy, pain, cravings, performance, or simply how you feel. Notice patterns without judgment. You're not grading yourself. You're gathering information. Keep what works. If a change helps you feel or perform better, keep it in your playbook. Discard what doesn't. Not every experiment succeeds. That's the point. Learning is progress.
- Try a qualitative experiment. Swap a pillow, change a light source, adjust a bedtime routine, or modify a meal. No data required — just awareness.

- Solve one nagging problem. Aches, sleep issues, digestion, stress, migraines — pick one and explore possible solutions.
- Build your own "lab notebook." A few notes on what you tried, what you noticed, and what you learned. Nothing fancy.

The Law of Experimentation is simple: When you treat your body like a laboratory, you stop fearing change. When you stop fearing change, you start learning. And when you start learning, you unlock the ability to age with intention.

Test, observe, adjust, repeat.

➤ IT'S NOT WHAT YOU KNOW, IT'S WHAT YOU DO. ➤

PART III SUMMARY — Learning from the Numbers

Part III has been about clarity — seeing your life through data rather than guesswork. These two laws — Measurement and Experimentation — give you the tools to understand what's really happening inside your body and inside your routines. Measurement shows you the truth. Experimentation helps you learn from it. Together, they turn your life into a feedback loop you can actually use.

When you track what matters, patterns emerge. You see which habits move the needle and which ones don't. You discover what your body responds to, what it resists, and what it needs. You stop relying on hope and start relying on evidence. And with each small experiment, you refine your approach, sharpen your decisions, and build a lifestyle that fits you — not someone else's blueprint.

Now that you've learned how to read your body's dashboard and adjust your course with intention, you're ready for the next layer: the mind behind the data. Part IV is about the beliefs, skills, and relationships that shape how you interpret your results, how you grow, and how you stay connected to the life you're building. It's where the numbers meet the narrative — and where your inner world begins to shape your outer experience.

PART IV — THE MIND

You've spent the last chapters learning how to understand your body — how to fuel it, move it, recover it, and then measure and experiment your way toward what works best for you. You've built a dashboard, run tests, and discovered what helps you feel and perform at your best. That work matters. It gives you the foundation for a long, healthy, intentional life.

But there's another layer — one that sits above all the data, all the routines, and all the experiments. It's the layer that determines how you interpret your experiences, how you respond to challenges, and how you navigate the inevitable ups and downs of aging.

It's your mind.

The next part of this book shifts from the physical to the psychological — from the mechanics of the body to the mechanics of meaning. Because no matter how strong, fit, or well-measured your body is, your mindset is the lens through which you experience everything.

And that lens can lift you up… or hold you down.

Every day, you carry a story about who you are, what you're capable of, and what your future holds. That story shapes your choices, your habits, your relationships, and your health. It influences how you age — not just physically, but emotionally and spiritually.

Chapter 8 is about that story.

It's about the Law of Mindset — the principle that attitude determines altitude. The way you think about aging shapes how you age. The beliefs you hold become the behaviors you practice. And the internal narrative you choose becomes the life you live.

You've learned how to experiment with your body.

Now it's time to learn how to experiment with your mind.

CHAPTER 8 — THE LAW OF MINDSET: ATTITUDE DETERMINES ALTITUDE

The law of mindset is simple: Your beliefs shape your behavior, and your behavior shapes your future.

I had read Lanny Bassham's book years earlier. If that name isn't familiar to you, Lanny won the silver medal in rifle shooting at the 1972 Olympics. Not being satisfied with that effort, he spent the next few years studying the best performers. Applying what he learned, he won gold in 1976. The following year, he formalized his Mental Management System and began coaching others.

I understood the theory of self-image — the idea that you can only perform up to the level you believe you can. I knew the words. I knew the concepts. I could have explained them to someone else. But nothing in my own life had changed.

Then I had lunch with Brian DeMott — master class competitor and former PSCA shooter.

I had reached out to Brian after watching him shoot sporting clays in competition on a couple of occasions. What stood out was how confident he looked as he prepared for each shot and how smoothly he executed each pair. I wasn't looking for a new coach. I simply wanted to interview him so I could share his experiences applying mental techniques with the readers of my blog.

I had prepared a list of questions, but two hours into the conversation, I realized I hadn't even taken the paper out of my pocket. We covered so much territory — taking care of aging parents, visualization, pushing through barriers, having a plan, transferring skills from one arena to another, confidence, performance regressing to the mean, and yes, self-image.

It wasn't until later that afternoon, when I sat down at my computer to write a blog post about our discussion, that something shifted.

As I unpacked everything we had talked about, it hit me with surprising force:

My progress wasn't being limited by my ability. It was being limited by my beliefs.

Brian didn't just know the Mental Management System — he lived it. He had implemented it, trained with it, and built his identity around it. And as I replayed our conversation, I realized something uncomfortable and liberating at the same time:

I had been treating self-image as information, not as a skill.

I had been reading about it, not practicing it.

I had been admiring the concept, not applying it.

Within two weeks, I had written my own self-image statement — something I had never done despite knowing the idea for years. And that moment taught me a lesson that has shaped every part of my life since:

It's not what you know.

It's what you do.

A few weeks later, I had my first on-course coaching session with Brian — now officially my coach. After watching me shoot a few targets, he said, "I am going to change your life." Little did he know, he already had.

Brian later told me that his own philosophy — the one that eventually shaped my tagline, "It's not what you know, it's what you do" — was influenced by a passage from the book of James (2:14–26). It's the idea that belief alone isn't enough; action is what gives belief its power.

That's the heart of mindset.

Zig Ziglar captured this truth in one line that has echoed through decades of personal development:

"Your attitude, not your aptitude, determines your altitude."

I had the aptitude. What I needed was the attitude.

And as I began paying attention, I noticed something else: the people who consistently performed well — whether in sports, business, relationships, or aging — weren't always the most talented. They were the ones who carried themselves with a certain posture toward life. A posture of possibility. A posture of resilience. A posture of curiosity.

Darrin Donnelly writes about this beautifully in his sports-fiction series. His characters succeed not because they are perfect, but because they choose an attitude that supports success. They choose optimism. They choose responsibility. They choose to respond rather than react. They choose to believe that improvement is possible.

That choice is the doorway to mindset.

World renowned Stanford University psychologist, Carol Dweck's research gives us the language: fixed mindset versus growth mindset.

A fixed mindset protects the ego.

A growth mindset builds capability.

A fixed mindset avoids challenge.

A growth mindset seeks it.

A fixed mindset fears failure.

A growth mindset learns from it.

And here's the connection that changed everything for me:

A growth mindset is the mental version of what you learned in Chapter 7. It's the belief that your mind is a laboratory, just as much as your body is.

That realization opened the door to the deeper work —
self-image, self-talk, identity, and the mental habits that shape

how we age. It led me back to Bassham's principles, to Brian's example, and to the understanding that the story you tell yourself becomes the life you live.

This chapter is about that story.

It's about the Law of Mindset — the principle that attitude determines altitude.

It's about the beliefs that lift you up or hold you down.

It's about the identity you practice every day, whether you realize it or not.

And it's about learning to shape your mind with the same intention you've brought to shaping your body.

Because aging well isn't just physical.

It's psychological.

It's emotional.

It's narrative.

And it begins with the mindset you choose.

Attitude

Attitude is the front door to mindset. It's the posture you bring into each day, the lens you use to interpret what happens to you, and the energy you project into the world. Long before you build a self-image statement or practice mental management skills, you choose an attitude — consciously or not.

One of the most powerful lessons I've learned is that attitude is not a personality trait. It's a decision. And like any decision, it can be trained.

Recall Darrin Donnelly's sports-fiction series mentioned earlier. His characters don't succeed because they are flawless or gifted. They succeed because they choose an attitude that supports success. They choose optimism when pessimism would be easier. They choose responsibility when excuses are available. They choose to respond rather than react. They choose to believe that improvement is possible.

Those choices are not dramatic. They're daily. And they compound.

That idea — that attitude is a choice — reminded me of a line from one of my favorite bands, Rush. In their song "Freewill", they make the point that even refusing to choose is still a choice. You can follow fear, you can follow external voices, or you can choose a clear path of your own. That message hit me hard the first time I heard it, and it has stayed with me ever since.

Attitude works the same way. You can choose a ready-made script about aging — the one society hands you — or you can choose your own. You can choose fear, resignation, and decline, or you can choose curiosity, capability, and growth. Either way, you're choosing.

I made one of those choices on my 59th birthday.

Something about that number hit me differently. I wasn't ready to "turn 60," not because of the number itself, but because of what I thought it implied — decline, slowing down, shrinking horizons. None of that matched how I felt or how I wanted to live.

So I made a decision: from that day forward, I would be "forever 59."

Not in a denial-of-aging way. Not in a "pretend I'm younger" way. But in a deliberate, intentional way. I wanted to keep developing wisdom — that part of aging I welcomed. But I didn't want my body or my mind to age in the ways we often assume they must. In fact, I wanted to roll some of it back if possible.

That decision became one of the attitudes that eventually made its way into my self-image statement. It wasn't about clinging to youth. It was about choosing a posture toward life — one of energy, curiosity, capability, and possibility. It was about refusing to let a number dictate my identity.

And here's the interesting part: once I chose that attitude, my behavior began to shift to match it.

I trained with more intention.

I recovered with more discipline.

I experimented more boldly.

I protected my mental inputs more carefully.

I carried myself differently — not younger, but more alive.

Attitude works that way. It sets the tone for everything that follows. It shapes the story you tell yourself before you ever write a self-image statement. It influences how you interpret setbacks, how you respond to challenges, and how you see your own potential.

When I look back, the "forever 59" decision wasn't about age at all. It was about identity. It was about choosing who I wanted to be and then living in alignment with that choice. It was the first time I realized that attitude is not just a feeling — it's a strategy.

And like any strategy, it can be refined, strengthened, and practiced.

That's why attitude comes first in this chapter. Before we talk about mindset, before we talk about self-image, before we talk about self-talk or stoicism or mental habits, we have to start with the simple truth:

Your attitude determines your altitude.

It determines how high you allow yourself to climb.

It determines how you interpret the world around you.

It determines how you age — physically, mentally, and emotionally.

Attitude is the doorway.

Mindset is what you build once you walk through it.

Mindset

If attitude is the posture you bring into each day, mindset is the operating system running underneath it. It's the set of beliefs you hold about your abilities, your potential, your limitations, and your future. Most people never examine their mindset. They assume their beliefs are simply "the way things are," when in reality, those beliefs are choices — often unconscious ones.

Carol Dweck's work gave me the language for something I had felt for years but couldn't articulate: the difference between a fixed mindset and a growth mindset.

A fixed mindset says, "This is who I am," "This is what I can do," and "This is what I can't do."

A growth mindset says, "I can learn," "I can adapt," and "I can improve."

A fixed mindset protects the ego.

A growth mindset builds capability.

A fixed mindset avoids challenge.

A growth mindset seeks it.

A fixed mindset fears failure.

A growth mindset learns from it.

When I first encountered Dweck's work, I saw myself in both columns. In some areas of life, I was wide open to growth. In others, I was quietly convinced that my best days were behind me. That's the tricky thing about mindset — it's not one belief, but a collection of beliefs, some empowering and some limiting.

But when I zoomed out and looked at my life, I realized something important: I had always been a serial hobbyist — someone who naturally gravitated toward learning new things.

I went from golf, to sailing, to racing sailboats.

Then to motorcycling.

Then, in my 50s, to shooting sporting clays — a sport I didn't even pick up until most people assume they're "too old" to start something new.

I even dabbled in learning to play the flute.

Each time, I was willing to be a beginner. I was willing to look awkward, feel unskilled, and start from scratch. I didn't call it a growth mindset back then — I just followed my curiosity. But looking back, that pattern was a clue: I was wired for growth, even if I didn't always apply it intentionally.

The clearest example came when I returned to school in my mid-50s.

I hadn't been in academia for more than 30 years. I was older than most of my classmates. I had a business to run, a family to support, and a full life already in motion. Everything about that decision should have triggered a fixed mindset — "I'm too old," "I'm too busy," "I don't belong here."

But something in me said, "Why not?"

And that simple question — that tiny spark of curiosity — opened the door to a completely different future.

Returning to school wasn't easy. I had to relearn how to study, how to write academic papers, how to manage deadlines, how to think critically in a structured environment. But each challenge reinforced the same truth: growth is available at any age if you're willing to pursue it.

That realization connected directly to what I had learned in Chapter 7:

Your body is a laboratory.

But so is your mind.

Once I started treating my mind as a place for experimentation, everything changed. I stopped assuming my reactions were fixed. I stopped assuming my limits were permanent. I stopped assuming that aging had to follow a predictable script.

Instead, I began asking questions:

- What if I could learn this?
- What if I could get better at that?
- What if I could change how I think about this situation?
- What if I could rewrite the story I've been telling myself?

This shift didn't happen all at once. It happened through small experiments — the same way physical change happens. I tried new routines. I tested new habits. I paid attention to how my mind responded to challenge, discomfort, and uncertainty. I noticed where I defaulted to fixed-mindset thinking and where I naturally embraced growth.

And I began to see something clearly:

Mindset is the bridge between attitude and self-image.

Attitude is the choice you make.

Mindset is the belief system that supports that choice.

Self-image is the identity that grows out of those beliefs.

When I chose to be "forever 59," that was attitude.

When I began believing I could improve physically and mentally at an age when many people assume decline, that was mindset.

When I wrote my self-image statement and started living it, that was identity.

Mindset sits right in the middle.

It's the belief that improvement is possible.

It's the belief that you can learn new skills at any age.

It's the belief that your best days aren't behind you.

It's the belief that aging is not a script — it's a story you get to write.

And once you adopt that belief, you begin to see opportunities everywhere. You start noticing where you've been holding yourself back. You start catching the quiet, limiting thoughts that shape your behavior. You start recognizing the moments when you default to old patterns. And you start choosing differently.

That's when mindset becomes powerful.

That's when it becomes personal.

That's when it becomes transformational.

And that's where self-image enters the picture — the deepest layer of all.

Self-Image

If attitude is the posture you choose and mindset is the belief system underneath it, then self-image is the identity you live from. It's the story you tell yourself about who you are and what you're capable of. And whether you realize it or not, that story shapes everything — your performance, your habits, your confidence, your aging, and your future.

Lanny Bassham's Mental Management System is built on a simple but profound idea: you cannot consistently outperform your self-image. You can have great technique, great equipment, great coaching, and great intentions — but if your self-image doesn't match the level you're trying to perform at, you will eventually regress to the identity you believe is "you."

I understood that concept intellectually when I first read Bassham's book. I could have explained it to someone else. But I didn't feel it. I didn't live it. I didn't apply it.

That changed after my lunch with Brian.

As I sat at my computer writing the blog post about our conversation, I realized that my self-image had quietly become outdated. It was built on old beliefs, old limitations, and old stories — many of which were no longer true. I had grown, but my self-image hadn't grown with me.

That realization was uncomfortable, but it was also liberating. Because if your self-image is just a story, then you can rewrite it.

Within two weeks, I had written my first self-image statement — at least as far as sporting clays goes. It wasn't perfect. It wasn't polished. But it was mine. And it was the first time I had ever taken the concept from theory to practice.

A Real Example: My First Self-Image Statement (June 3, 2021)

When I wrote my first self-image statement, I didn't know exactly what it should look like. I just knew I needed to write it in the present tense, as though I were already living the identity I wanted to grow into. This is what I came up with:

> My name is Mike Rouleau. I am a Master Class shotgunner.
>
> I achieved Master Class status in the fall of 2023 after reaching AA in the spring of 2022. Being a Master Class shooter lends credibility to my mental skills blog, where I gain tremendous satisfaction sharing sport psychology tips with amateur athletes around the world.
>
> Moving up to Master Class required improving my target-kill percentage from 72.6% to 85%. It is now like me to break more than 90% on most courses in competition. This was accomplished through a series of goals. I worked diligently with my shooting coach at least six times per year. I kept my weight below 160 pounds

> and maintained upper-body strength through a daily exercise routine. I increased my deliberate practice sessions from two per month to a minimum of four. At home, I practiced meditation at least three times per week and eye-training once per week. I engaged in mental practice each night. I refined my pre- and post-match routines, as well as my pre- and post-shot routines, and applied them every time.
>
> I am a Master Class shotgunner. When I enter a shooting stand, I am confident in my knowledge and abilities to break every target presented to me — whether it is the first pair or the final pair of a station.

This wasn't who I was at the time.

It was who I was becoming.

And writing it in the present tense made that identity feel real, long before the results showed up.

That's the power of a self-image statement. It lets you live your future in the present, so your behavior begins to align with the identity you're building.

Why Writing a Self-Image Statement Works

In one of my blog posts, I explained that writing a self-image statement forces you to clarify four essential elements of success:

- What you want to accomplish
- Why it matters to you
- How you're going to achieve it
- When you will achieve it

Most people never articulate these four things. They drift. They hope. They react. A self-image statement pulls all of that into focus. It becomes a personal blueprint — a clear declaration of who you are becoming and how you intend to get there.

My sporting clays statement did exactly that. It defined the identity I wanted, the reasons behind it, the habits required to support it, and the timeline I expected to see change. Did it all happen per the plan? Almost. I did achieve AA status — but this brings up a very important point.

Your self-image can and should evolve as your life expands.

Not when things get difficult and you want an "out," but when your world gets bigger and your identity grows with it.

In my case, sporting clays remains an important part of my self-image, but it no longer holds the same prominence it once did. My self-image has grown larger, broader, and more aligned with the person I'm becoming — someone focused on the full spectrum of becoming a super-ager.

How to Write a Self-Image Statement

Bassham's method is simple, but powerful. A self-image statement is written as identity, but identity naturally includes both the process you live by and the outcomes that are normal for someone with that identity. The key is that outcomes are framed as expressions of who you are — not wishes for who you hope to become.

1. Write in the present tense

Not "I will be confident," but "I am confident."

Not "I hope to be consistent," but "I am a consistent performer."

Your brain responds to present-tense identity statements. It begins aligning your behavior to match the story you're telling.

2. Describe the identity you want to live from

Identity comes first. Results follow from identity.

Examples:

- "I am calm and composed under pressure."
- "I am a disciplined athlete."
- "I am improving every week."
- "I am someone who takes care of my body and mind."

3. Include outcomes only as expressions of identity

A self-image statement is not a list of goals or fantasies. But it can include outcomes — as long as they are framed as normal for someone with your identity.

For example, in my sporting clays statement, I wrote:

"It is now like me to break more than 90% on most courses in competition."

That line works because it isn't a wish. It's a description of what is typical for the identity I'm stepping into. It reinforces the story — it doesn't replace it.

4. Keep it positive and specific

Avoid "don't," "stop," or "never." The brain doesn't respond well to negation.

Instead of "I don't get nervous," write:

"I am steady and focused."

5. Make it believable — but slightly beyond your current self

Self-image grows at the edge of your comfort zone.

Not fantasy.

Not delusion.

Just the next version of you.

6. Read it daily — and make it impossible to forget

Self-image grows through repetition — what you picture, say, and feel.

When I wrote my first self-image statement, I didn't trust myself to remember to read it. So, I made it unavoidable. I printed three copies:

- One in my bathroom vanity — I read it every morning and every night while brushing my teeth.
- One on my desk — a reminder before I started work each day.
- One in my truck — so I could read it before practice or a competition.

Those three copies weren't decoration. They were anchors. They kept my identity front-and-center. They made the new story familiar. They made the new identity feel normal.

A Note on Bassham's Work

Everything I've shared here is just the surface. Lanny Bassham's Mental Management System is a deep, well-developed framework, and if this chapter resonates with you, his books and training materials are the best place to learn the full method. What I'm offering is my personal experience applying a small part of his system — not a substitute for his work.

Self-image is powerful because it's personal. It's the story you tell yourself when no one is listening. It's the voice that whispers "you can" or "you can't." It's the ceiling you set — or the ceiling you remove.

And that brings us to the next layer: self-talk — the language of self-image.

Self-Talk

Self-talk is the language of your identity. It's the running commentary in your mind — the words you use to explain your experiences, evaluate your performance, and interpret your world. And whether you realize it or not, those words shape your physiology, your emotions, your confidence, and your behavior.

Lanny Bassham teaches that self-image grows through three channels: what you picture, what you say, and what you feel. Self-talk is the "what you say" part — and it's often the most powerful. It's how you reinforce the identity you're building.

But not all self-talk is helpful. Some of it is chatter.

When Self-Talk Turns Against You

In his book *Chatter*, Ethan Kross explains that the inner voice isn't always your ally. Under pressure or stress, it can catastrophize, criticize, and spiral. And the body reacts to this almost instantly.

Research shows that harsh first-person self-talk — "I can't believe I did that," "I always screw this up," "I'm such an idiot" — causes immediate physiological changes. Blood vessels constrict. Stress hormones spike. The amygdala, the brain's threat center, activates. Your body shifts into fight-or-flight.

Self-talk isn't just psychological.

It's biological.

It changes your body in real time.

Kross shares a story about receiving a threatening letter after a TV appearance. He spiraled into fear and rumination — until he tried something counterintuitive.

He stopped using "I."

He started talking to himself using his own name.

And the shift was immediate.

Distanced Self-Talk

Kross calls this technique distanced self-talk — switching from first person ("I") to second person ("you") or even third person (your own name). It creates just enough psychological space to calm the emotional storm.

Instead of:

"I can't handle this."

You say:

"Mike, you've handled things like this before."

Instead of:

"I always fall apart under pressure."

You say:

"You know how to breathe, reset, and execute."

This tiny shift:

- reduces emotional intensity
- increases self-control
- calms your physiology

And it works fast — often within seconds.

The Best-Friend Standard

Distanced self-talk is powerful, but I added one more rule for myself — one that changed everything:

I only talk to myself the way I would talk to my best friend.

If my best friend missed a target, I wouldn't say, "You idiot."

I'd say, "Reset. You know what to do."

If my best friend was struggling, I wouldn't say, "You're too old for this."

I'd say, "You've reinvented yourself before. You can do it again."

If my best friend was frustrated, I wouldn't say, "You're never going to get this right."

I'd say, "Keep going. You're closer than you think."

This standard keeps my self-talk grounded, compassionate, and constructive. It prevents me from slipping into the kind of harsh chatter that shuts down performance and erodes confidence. And it aligns perfectly with the identity I'm trying to reinforce through my self-image statement.

A Simple Awareness Experiment

One of the fastest ways to improve your self-talk is to measure it. Not analyze it. Not judge it. Just notice it.

For a few days:

- keep a small notebook and pencil with you
- make a tick mark every time you catch positive self-talk
- make a tick mark every time you catch negative self-talk

No sentences. No explanations.

Just marks.

Most people are shocked by what they discover.

Some realize they're far kinder to themselves than they thought.

Others realize they're carrying a constant stream of quiet criticism.

Almost everyone realizes they've been running on autopilot.

And here's the magic:

awareness alone begins to change the behavior.

When you know you're going to make a tick mark, you become more aware of the tone you're using. You catch yourself sooner. You redirect faster. You start applying the best-friend standard automatically.

Do this for several days and you'll see the ratio shift — not because you're forcing it, but because awareness itself is transformative.

Your Spoken Words Count Too

There's one more layer that often gets overlooked:

the rules for internal self-talk apply to the words you speak out loud.

Your subconscious doesn't distinguish between:

- what you think
- what you mutter under your breath
- what you say to a friend
- what you say about yourself in frustration
- what you joke about
- what you repeat often enough to sound "true"

It absorbs all of it.

If you say, "I'm terrible at this," your subconscious hears it.

If you say, "I'm too old for that," your subconscious hears it.

If you say, "I always choke under pressure," your subconscious hears it.

And it begins to build an identity around those statements.

That's why I try to keep my spoken words aligned with the same standard I use for my internal dialogue:

If I wouldn't say it to someone I care about, I don't say it to myself — not in my head, and not out loud.

This simple rule keeps my identity aligned, my emotions steady, and my self-image growing in the direction I've chosen. With a little practice, positive self-talk has become my super-power. It can for you too.

Self-talk is how you reinforce your identity.

It's how you strengthen your beliefs.

It's how you shape the story you live inside.

Applied Mindset Skills

Mindset isn't something you think about once and forget. It's something you practice. And the practices that shape your mindset are the same ones that shape how you age — how you respond to stress, how you interpret challenges, how you recover from setbacks, and how you carry yourself through the world.

These are the applied skills that turn mindset into a way of living.

Stoicism: Respond, Don't React

Stoicism has become one of the most practical mindset tools in my life, especially as I've gotten older. At its core, Stoicism teaches one simple principle: you control your response, not the world. You don't control other people, the weather, your genetics, or the randomness of life — but you do control your interpretation, your effort, your habits, and your identity.

Ryan Holiday has done more than anyone in recent years to make Stoicism accessible and actionable. His four-part series on the Stoic virtues — Courage, Discipline, Justice, and Wisdom — reframes ancient philosophy into daily practices. Each virtue becomes a lesson for how to live well, age well, and respond well.

- Courage reminds you to step into challenges instead of shrinking from them.
- Discipline keeps your habits aligned with your goals, especially when motivation fades.
- Justice pushes you to act with integrity and contribute to something larger than yourself.
- Wisdom helps you see clearly, choose well, and avoid unnecessary suffering.

These aren't abstract ideas. They're daily behaviors. And as I've aged, I've found that these virtues become more important, not less. They help you stay grounded, intentional, and resilient.

Holiday's *Daily Stoic* is another tool I return to often — short reflections paired with ancient Stoic passages. For one solid year, I kept this book on my desk and read each day's entry. Most days, it made me pause and reflect on some aspect of my life — and very often, it nudged me toward a small but meaningful change. Since finishing the book, I now turn to Holiday's daily email for more inspiration. And yes, I'll pull the book out again and work through it for another year. A new year brings new interpretation to familiar ideas.

And then there's Marcus Aurelius.

His *Meditations* — or Reflections, as Holiday often calls them — is one of the most remarkable books ever written. A Roman emperor, writing private notes to himself about humility, mortality, discipline, and purpose. He wasn't writing for an audience. He was writing to stay sane, centered, and grounded in a world he couldn't fully control.

There's something powerful about that — a man with absolute power reminding himself daily to stay calm, stay kind, stay disciplined, stay present.

As I've gotten older, I've found myself returning to Marcus Aurelius more often. Not because I want to be philosophical, but because I want to be steady. I want to respond instead of react. I want to focus on what I can control and let go of what I can't. I want to age with intention, not anxiety.

Stoicism gives you that.

It's not about suppressing emotion.

It's about directing it.

It's about choosing your response.

It's about living from the inside out.

And when you combine Stoicism with the self-image and self-talk work from earlier in the chapter, you get a mindset that is both resilient and compassionate — a mindset that supports aging well, performing well, and living well.

Enjoyment as a Skill

Almost thirty years ago, I found myself in a vicious loop. I was suffering from weekly, sometimes daily migraines. To prevent them, I was taking a prescription medication (Inderal). Over time, the medication caused laxity in the valve at the top of my stomach, allowing acid to creep up into my esophagus. Eventually, the acid began eroding my larynx, creating a painful ulcer.

To heal, I had to stop eating spicy foods, drinking alcohol, and consuming caffeine. I also had to stop the Inderal. I was terrified to think what would happen to my migraines without the medication.

And then something surprising happened:

when I cleaned up my diet, the migraines went away — or at least became far less frequent.

My lifestyle choices had contributed to the migraines, which required a medication that changed my physiology in a negative way, which caused the ulcer. When I stopped the behaviors and treated the ulcer properly, it healed.

On my final visit to the ENT doctor, he surprised me by pulling out his prescription pad. I thought I was done with meds. He wrote something, tore the sheet off, and handed it to me.

It said simply:

"Enjoy Life."

Powerful stuff.

Most people think enjoyment is something that just happens. I've learned it's something you can train.

Enjoyment grows. when you:

- notice small wins
- savor moments
- stay present
- celebrate progress
- choose gratitude over comparison

This isn't about pretending everything is great. It's about recognizing that joy is a form of fuel — and as we age, we need more of it, not less.

Enjoyment keeps you engaged.

Engagement keeps you young.

Intentional Media Diet

Your mind is shaped by what you consume — just like your body is shaped by what you eat.

As I got older, I realized I couldn't afford to let my attention be hijacked by:

- outrage
- fear
- noise
- endless scrolling
- other people's priorities

So I became intentional about my inputs:

- more books, fewer feeds
- less TV and internet news, more real-world experiences
- more learning, less reacting

I mentioned earlier that the average adult watches 3.7 hours of TV a day. We have a rule about TV time in our house: it's done with intention. We don't have the TV on as background noise. It's not on during dinner. It's not running just to fill silence. It's on when there is something we've decided we want to watch — and yes, that can include Columbo reruns or my favorite hockey team — but always on our schedule, not the other way around.

This isn't about avoiding the world.

It's about choosing what deserves space in your mind.

Aging well requires protecting your mental environment.

Protecting Your Attention

Attention is the currency of your life.

Where it goes, your energy follows.

Where your energy goes, your identity follows.

As I've gotten older, I've become more protective of:

- my schedule
- my focus
- my emotional bandwidth

- my creative time
- my recovery time

Protecting your attention isn't selfish.

It's strategic.

It's how you ensure your best energy goes to the things that matter most.

Wearing the Uniform

This is one of my favorite applied mindset skills — and one of the simplest.

"Wearing the uniform" means acting like the person you want to become before you fully feel like that person.

A few examples from my life:

- Cycling gear. During COVID, I bought a new bike — carbon frame, great drivetrain, lightweight and fast. I started riding longer distances, and a few weeks later, my butt hurt. I went back to the shop asking for a new saddle. The salesperson asked what I was wearing. I admitted: gym shorts. She suggested padded cycling shorts. I always thought they looked silly. Turns out the only silly thing was me. The right gear changed everything. I wasn't just someone who biked — I became a cyclist.

- My first triathlon. I learned my lesson. When I signed up for my first triathlon, my wife helped me pick out a real tri-suit — one garment that worked for the swim, bike, and run. I wasn't a poser. I was a triathlete.
- Dress for success. In business, showing up confidently matters. The uniform helps you step into the role.
- Aging intentionally. Now, I practice carrying myself like someone who is aging with purpose — whether I'm at the gym or anywhere else.

Identity is reinforced by behavior.

When you "wear the uniform," you're signaling to your brain:

This is who we are now.

And your brain listens.

Choosing Inputs That Shape Identity

Everything you allow into your life — people, habits, routines, conversations, environments — is shaping your identity in real time.

As I moved into my 50s and 60s, I became more selective about:

- who I spend time with
- what I read
- what I watch
- what I listen to

- what I practice
- what I tolerate

Aging well isn't passive.

It's intentional.

You're always becoming someone.

The question is whether you're choosing who that someone is.

Bringing It All Together

These applied mindset skills are the bridge between the inner work — attitude, mindset, self-image, self-talk — and the outer life you're building as you age.

They help you:

- stay grounded
- stay intentional
- stay engaged
- stay aligned
- stay young in the ways that matter

Aging well isn't about resisting time.

It's about shaping who you become as time passes.

Chapter Summary: Mindset, Self-Image, and Applied Skills

The law of mindset is simple: Your beliefs shape your behavior, and your behavior shapes your future.

- Mindset is practiced, not inherited. Your daily responses, interpretations, and habits shape how you age.
- Attitude is your posture. You choose how you show up, especially when life gets messy.
- Mindset is your belief system. It determines how you interpret challenges and what you expect from yourself.
- Self-image is your identity. You cannot consistently outperform the story you believe about yourself.
- Self-image grows through repetition. What you picture, say, and feel becomes who you are.
- Write your identity in the present tense. Describe the person you are becoming as though you already are that person.
- Include outcomes only as expressions of identity. Not wishes — normal behaviors for the version of you that you're stepping into.
- Read your self-image daily. Make it unavoidable. Identity grows through exposure.
- Self-talk is the language of identity. It shapes your physiology, your emotions, and your performance.
- Use distanced self-talk. "You've got this" or "Mike, reset" calms the brain and restores control.

- Apply the best-friend standard. Never speak to yourself in a way you wouldn't speak to someone you love.
- Track your self-talk. Notice the ratio of positive to negative. Awareness alone begins to shift the pattern.
- Your spoken words matter. Your subconscious learns from what you say out loud.
- Stoicism teaches response over reaction. Focus on what you can control — your effort, your habits, your interpretation.
- Virtues become practices. Courage, Discipline, Justice, and Wisdom help you age with steadiness and intention.
- Enjoyment is a skill. Savoring, noticing, and celebrating keep you engaged — and engagement keeps you young.
- Curate your media diet. Protect your mental environment from noise, outrage, and distraction.
- Guard your attention. Where your attention goes, your identity follows.
- Wear the uniform. Act like the person you want to become; behavior reinforces identity.
- Choose inputs that shape who you're becoming. People, habits, routines, and environments all sculpt your future self.

- Aging well isn't about resisting time. It's about shaping who you become as time passes.

Your Turn — Practice the Mindset That Shapes Who You Become

- Write your self-image statement. Use present-tense identity language. Describe the person you are becoming as though you already are that person. Read it every day. Morning and night. Make it unavoidable.
- Track your self-talk. For the next three days, carry a small notebook. Make a tick mark for every positive and negative moment you notice.
- Use distanced self-talk. When pressure rises, switch to "you" or your own name.
- Apply the best-friend standard. Speak to yourself only in ways you would speak to someone you care about.
- Choose one Stoic practice this week. A morning reflection, an evening review, or a single virtue to focus on.
- Train enjoyment. Notice one small win or moment to savor each day.
- Prune and nurture your inputs. Remove one source of noise and add one source of nourishment.

- Protect your attention. Block off one hour for focused work, reflection, or recovery — and guard it.
- Wear the uniform. Choose one behavior or posture that reflects the identity you're building.

Aging well is not an accident. It's a practice. And it begins with the mindset you choose today. And now you know where the tag line at the end of every chapter got its origination:

➤ IT'S NOT WHAT YOU KNOW, IT'S WHAT YOU DO. ➤

By now, you've built the internal foundation: your attitude, your mindset, your self-image, your self-talk, and the daily practices that shape who you're becoming. You've learned how to direct your thoughts, protect your attention, and carry yourself with intention as you age.

But mindset alone isn't enough.

A strong mind needs something to grow toward.

Identity needs new material to work with.

Aging well requires staying curious, adaptable, and mentally alive.

That's where we're headed next.

Chapter 9 is about The Law of Lifelong Learning — the idea that your brain, your skills, and your potential don't have an expiration date. It's about choosing growth over stagnation, curiosity over comfort, and possibility over decline. It's about keeping your mind young by continually feeding it, challenging it, and stretching it.

If mindset is the engine, learning is the fuel.

Let's turn the page and explore how lifelong learning becomes one of the most powerful tools for aging well.

CHAPTER 9 — THE LAW OF LIFELONG LEARNING

The law of lifelong learning is simple: A growing mind is a younger mind.

"If what this guy is selling costs less than $100, I'm in."

That was my actual thought about 90 minutes into an infomercial I somehow got sucked into watching one rainy afternoon about a decade ago. I was sitting at my computer — probably checking the weather — when a video popped up. And instead of clicking away like I always do, I kept watching.

What had me so hooked that I was ready to part with a crisp Benjamin Franklin?

Maybe you saw it too. It seemed to appear every time I loaded a webpage back then. It was a long-form pitch from internet entrepreneur Tai Lopez promoting his program The 67 Steps, a 67-day guide to what he called "the good life" — health, wealth, love, and happiness. And honestly, who doesn't want those four pillars?

I never — and I repeat, never — watch these kinds of ads. Yet here I was, fully invested, nodding along, and waiting for the price reveal like it was the climax of an action-thriller movie. Was it the Lamborghini in his garage? His enthusiasm? The promise of those four pillars? I still don't know. What I do know is that when he finally announced the price — $67 for 67 days of lessons — I clicked "Buy Now" without hesitation.

You might think this was a little frivolous. Call it an experiment. Better yet, call it a successful experiment.

Each day, I watched a one-hour video lesson and even took notes, eventually filling a binder I kept on my desk for years. During the program, I had to travel, and rather than miss a day, I emailed the support team and asked for early access to a few lessons. They obliged. (If you're not hearing my kids' violins playing in the background, you may want to revisit Chapter 4 on staying motivated.)

Did I find the holy grail of health, wealth, love, and happiness? Probably not. But I did gain some valuable insights. A few of Tai's ideas helped me make specific improvements in my business — enough to more than pay back the $67. But the biggest gift was something else entirely:

Tai got me interested in reading again.

And that single shift — rediscovering the power of books — changed the trajectory of my learning, my mindset, and ultimately, how I age.

The Power of Books

Before Tai launched his 67 Steps program, he had already built a following around one bold idea: he read a book a day. Yes — a book a day. I liken that to riding my bike 10,000 miles a year: something I might do once, but not something I'd want to make a habit of. But the fire was lit. And Tai provided the starter fuel for my own re-engagement with lifelong learning through reading.

He posted his list of all-time favorite books — ranked, updated periodically, and spanning an incredible range of topics. Suddenly, I had a shopping list. And it didn't disappoint. His list covered everything from business success to nutrition, from philosophy to personal development. A true soup-to-nuts collection of ideas worth putting into your mind.

I couldn't read a book a day like Tai claimed to, but I could read a book a week. And I've continued that practice to this day. (Okay, sometimes it's a book every other week — but the spirit is there.) The point wasn't speed. The point was re-opening the door to learning.

Tai explained something that stuck with me: books are a way to access mentors from every walk of life, across every era, without ever leaving your living room. Where else can you tap into the wisdom of people both living and dead — from Warren Buffett on business (who, by the way, spends several hours a day reading — coincidence he's been so successful?) to Marcus Aurelius on how to live a steady, Stoic life?

But Tai didn't just reignite my interest in reading. He taught me how to really read a book.

He encouraged starting with the table of contents to understand the structure and the promise of the book. Then reading the conclusion to see where the author is trying to take you. Then flipping through the opening and closing paragraphs of each chapter to get a preview of the ideas before diving in. It was a simple system, but it changed the way I approached every book thereafter. Instead of reading passively, I was reading with intention — looking for the ideas that mattered, the insights that could shape my thinking, and the lessons I could apply.

That shift — from casual reading to intentional reading — was transformative. It wasn't just about consuming information. It was about building a lifelong habit of learning, one book at a time.

A Few Final Thoughts on Books

I love books. I love the way they feel in my hands. I love being able to glance at the pages and instantly know how far along I am. There's something timeless about them.

Speaking of timeless, I was fortunate to travel to Mainz, Germany for work a few years back. Wandering along the riverfront near my hotel, I stumbled across the Gutenberg Museum — complete with replicas of the first mechanical printing press developed around 1450. I joined a tour that had just started. I'm not even sure what language it was in, but it didn't matter. Watching those replicas in action was astonishing. We take cheap books for granted today, but it wasn't always that way.

And now, of course, there's an even cheaper way to get words into our brains: e-readers.

I resisted that technological shift until last year (that high-tech/high-touch tension again). I still prefer bound books, but when the price difference is significant, I go with the e-reader. And honestly, learning how to use the device was its own little brain workout.

Reading is one area of our household budget that has no limit. My wife and I treat it as an investment, not a cost. Keeping our brains young is worth far more than anything we could possibly spend on books.

As for choosing what to read, there are endless recommendations online — like Tai's list I mentioned earlier — but I strongly suggest venturing outside your usual interests. I gravitate toward non-fiction and how-to books, but I sprinkle in history and fiction as well. One of the best ways to do this is to let a friend or relative pick a few books for you. My wife is especially good at this. She often gives me books for my birthday or Christmas — ones I never would have chosen myself.

I have a little system: I rank the books in order of which ones I think I'll like most and read those first, leaving the "bottom of the pile" for last. And wouldn't you know it — those bottom-of-the-pile books often end up being some of the most enjoyable ones I've read. So learn from my bad behavior and push yourself to read outside your comfort zone.

And what if you start a book and it just isn't speaking to you? Put it down. Come back to it later. It might resonate more at another time — or it might not. Either is fine. You don't owe the author anything. You already paid them. Your debt is cleared. I've only abandoned one book in my life, and I'm still waiting for the right time to appreciate it.

Learning Through Teaching — Why Explaining What You Read Works

One of the most powerful tools I discovered for cementing what I read came from my days working on my psychology degree. As I read a book (or an academic paper), I would explain the key ideas to my wife. It's one thing to passively read material; it's an entirely different experience to explain it to another person. Teaching forces clarity. It exposes gaps. It demands comprehension at a deeper level.

I suppose that's part of the allure of a book club. The act of discussing what you've read transforms the material from information into understanding.

A side benefit of this approach is that my wife gets to enjoy the highlights of my reading. And she reciprocates by explaining to me the latest video she's watched online. This strategy really works. I have hundreds of books on my shelves (plural), but the ones I remember best are the ones we talked about on our evening walks or over dinner.

Games, Play, and Keeping the Brain Young

Speaking of my wife, another way we keep our brains engaged is by playing games. Our current favorite is Bananagrams. It's a word puzzle similar to Scrabble, but with a twist: speed matters. You have to use all your tiles before your opponent does. Our games are friendly — but competitive in a very loving way (mostly).

And the science backs this up. Activities that require attention, focus, and engagement help maintain cognitive fitness as we age. The brain's ability to adapt and rewire itself, neuroplasticity, is central to staying mentally sharp, and mentally stimulating games can support that process. Harvard Health notes that engaging in mentally challenging activities helps preserve and even enhance cognitive function as we age.

UCLA Health also highlights that brain-training games can help delay age-related cognitive decline by challenging memory, focus, and problem-solving skills — exactly the kind of demands games like Bananagrams create.

And broader research shows that structured cognitive training, especially when combined with physical activity and social engagement, can significantly improve cognitive performance in adults over 50 with effects lasting up to a decade.

In other words: play is not frivolous. It's fuel for a healthy, adaptable brain.

Writing Into the Brain

Did you learn how to study in high school?

No?

Me either.

When I got to NC State, I quickly realized I needed a better way to lock information into my head. The application process I described earlier may have been trivial, but the workload in engineering school wasn't. I was challenged academically for the first time. (Okay, full disclosure: there was that "C" on my health education final exam in 8th grade… but does that really count now?)

So what was the silver bullet that saved my bacon and helped me graduate with honors?

Listening — really listening — and writing down the essence of what I heard.

Not copying every word. Not transcribing the lecture. But paying attention, distilling the key ideas, and making cogent notes in my own words. I discovered that what I heard and then wrote down was cemented into my memory. I could take notes, ball up the paper, throw it away — and the information was still there. Its job was done. I had etched it into my brain.

That habit never left me.

How I Do It Now: I Blog

Today, I write to learn. I have a blog about mental skills for the amateur athlete. Why? Because it's a topic I'm genuinely interested in. It's something I want to keep learning about. I don't pretend to know everything — far from it — but I'm eager to explore, experiment, and share what I discover.

And here's the magic:

When I learn something new and then write about it, the learning sticks.

I'm not trying to make a dime from the blog. I don't run ads. There are no subscription fees. I personally pay the hosting costs. It's a labor of love, and a powerful way to keep my brain young. Honestly, just figuring out how to set up the blog was a tremendous learning opportunity.

And if you're thinking, "I bet you're doing the same thing with this book," you'd be right.

Writing a Book Is a Mental Gym

Writing a book is a major brain exercise. It forces clarity. It demands structure. It requires you to wrestle with ideas until they make sense — not just to you, but to someone else reading your words.

And here's the best part:

Anyone can do it.

You don't need a degree. You don't need permission. You don't need a publisher. You just need curiosity, a willingness to learn, and the courage to share what you've learned. These same ingredients fueled my studying in college, my blogging, and now this book.

But what if you want something more formal or structured in your learning?

That's where we're headed next.

Formal Education and Structured Learning

I wanted the degree. I've already explained how I went back to school in my 50s, and I'm quite sure I could do it again now in my 60s. As far as I know, there's no age limit on a school application. I don't claim to have any special skills that made it easier for me to re-enter formal education more than three decades after my last classroom experience. I simply decided to do it — and then did the work.

And I wasn't the only one in my household to take that leap. After I earned my master's degree, my wife decided to return to school herself. She insists she wasn't trying to upstage me, but a couple of years later I found myself sitting in a very large auditorium, watching with enormous pride as she received her PhD in Health Sciences. Yes, she may have been the oldest in her graduating class, but she also brought more to her cohort because of her lived experience and maturity. Everyone won.

Today, the options for formal learning are almost limitless. If you don't like a traditional classroom environment, pursue an online degree. If you don't like online learning and prefer raising your hand in person instead of clicking a Zoom icon, go the traditional route. There are hybrid systems too. Don't want the pressure of grades? Audit a class. Community colleges, local universities, online programs, some of the best institutions in the world put their courses online, often for cheap or even free.

Pick something you like and give it a try.

And don't limit yourself to academic pursuits. I mentioned earlier that I love the sound of the flute. I call my wife "Ann the Enabler". I casually mentioned I was interested in learning the flute, and one appeared on my desk. Ballroom dancing, beekeeping, Mahjong, photography, AI and PC skills, the list of things you can learn is endless. I've said before that I'm a serial hobbyist, always starting over, always learning something new.

Your local community center probably has a catalog full of classes you've never even considered. There are so many ways to structure an education and keep your brain engaged, happy, and young.

The Many Paths of Lifelong Learning

By now you can see that lifelong learning isn't one thing. It's not just reading books, or going back to school, or picking up a new hobby. It's a mosaic, a collection of practices that keep your brain active, curious, and engaged.

Books were my re-entry point. They reopened the door to curiosity and gave me access to mentors I never would have met otherwise. Teaching what I read, whether to my wife on our evening walks or to myself through note-taking, deepened my understanding and locked the ideas into my memory. Games like Bananagrams added another layer, challenging my brain in a playful, social way that science shows help maintain cognitive flexibility.

Blogging became a different kind of classroom, one where I learned by writing, by wrestling with ideas, and by sharing what I discovered. It wasn't about making money or building an audience. It was about keeping my mind sharp and staying connected to a topic I care about.

Formal education reminded me that age has nothing to do with the ability to learn. I went back to school in my 50s. My wife earned her PhD shortly before turning 60. Today, learning is more accessible than ever — online, in person, hybrid, graded, audited, free, paid, structured, or casual. There is a format for every personality and every season of life.

And then there are the hobbies — the flute, photography, ballroom dancing, beekeeping, Mahjong, technology skills. These aren't just pastimes. They are brain workouts disguised as fun. They stretch you. They humble you. They remind you what it feels like to be a beginner again — which is one of the healthiest states a brain can be in.

Taken together, these experiences form a simple truth:

Lifelong learning is not a single habit. It's a lifestyle.

It's the willingness to stay open, to stay curious, to stay engaged with the world. It's the decision to keep expanding your identity rather than letting it shrink. It's the belief that your best thinking, your best creativity, and your best growth can still be ahead of you.

And now that we've explored the many ways learning can show up in your life, we can bring it all together into something practical — a simple, sustainable way to build your own lifelong learning practice.

Chapter Summary: Building Your Lifelong Learning Practice

By now, you've seen that learning can take many forms — books, conversations, games, writing, formal education, hobbies, and everything in between. The real question becomes: How do you turn all of this into a sustainable practice? Not a phase. Not a burst of enthusiasm. A way of living.

The good news is that a lifelong learning practice doesn't require a rigid schedule or a color-coded planner. It simply requires intention — a decision to keep your brain in motion.

A few principles make all the difference:

- Feed your curiosity regularly. You don't need to devour a book a day. A chapter, a few pages, a podcast, a documentary, a conversation — they all count. Curiosity is a muscle; use it and it grows.
- Mix your inputs. Read widely. Play games. Take a class. Try a new hobby. Write about what you're learning. Each channel lights up a different part of

the brain, and the variety keeps you mentally flexible.

- Teach what you learn. Explain a concept to a spouse, a friend, or even to yourself in a journal. Teaching forces clarity and deepens understanding. It's one of the most powerful learning tools available.
- Stay a beginner. Pick up something new every so often — a musical instrument, a language, a craft, a sport, a technology skill. Being a beginner keeps you humble, curious, and neurologically young.
- Follow your energy, not your guilt. If a book isn't speaking to you, put it down. If a class feels wrong, switch. If a hobby loses its spark, try another. Learning should feel like exploration, not obligation.
- Invest in your mind. Whether it's books, classes, tools, or time, treat learning as an investment — one that pays dividends in resilience, creativity, confidence, and joy.
- Keep it playful. Games, puzzles, friendly competition, creative projects — these aren't distractions. They're brain training disguised as fun. Play is one of the most underrated learning tools we have.

When you weave these elements together, something powerful happens: learning stops being an event and becomes a lifestyle.

You stop thinking of yourself as someone who used to learn and start seeing yourself as someone who is always learning.

And that identity — the identity of a learner — is one of the strongest predictors of healthy aging. It keeps your world expanding. It keeps your brain adaptable. It keeps your spirit engaged. It keeps you young.

The practice doesn't have to be perfect. It just has to be yours.

Every time you stretch yourself — through reading, teaching, playing, writing, studying, or trying something new — you signal to your brain that you are still in motion. And motion, in all its forms, is the antidote to aging.

Your Turn

Lifelong learning doesn't require a classroom, a degree, or a grand plan. It requires a posture — curiosity, openness, and the willingness to keep expanding who you are. A few simple steps can help you build your own practice. Pick a few from the following list:

- Choose one book you've been meaning to read — or ask someone you trust to pick one for you. Start with ten minutes a day.
- Teach one idea you've learned recently to someone else — a spouse, a friend, a coworker, or even to yourself in a journal.

- Add one playful challenge to your week — a puzzle, a game, a brain teaser, something that makes you think and smile at the same time.
- Write something down — a reflection, a summary, a blog post, a note to yourself. Writing is thinking made visible.
- Try one new skill — a class, a hobby, a musical instrument, a craft, a technology tool. Let yourself be a beginner again.
- Invest in your mind — set aside a small, guilt-free budget for books, classes, or tools that support your growth.

These aren't tasks to complete. They're invitations. Each one reinforces the identity that matters most for aging well:

I am someone who keeps learning.

When you adopt that identity — even in small, imperfect ways — your world stays open, your brain stays adaptable, and your life stays rich with possibility.

The law of lifelong learning is simple: A growing mind is a younger mind.

➤ IT'S NOT WHAT YOU KNOW, IT'S WHAT YOU DO. ➤

Lifelong learning keeps the mind young, flexible, and open. But there's another truth I've discovered as I've aged: learning is only half the story. Growth doesn't happen in isolation. It happens in relationships — in the people we meet, the communities we join, the conversations we have, and the connections we choose to nurture.

You can read all the books in the world, take all the classes, master all the hobbies, and sharpen your mind in every way imaginable. But if you do it alone, something essential is missing. We are wired for connection. We thrive when we belong. We grow when we are seen, supported, challenged, and loved.

If lifelong learning keeps your mind alive, connection keeps your spirit alive.

And just like learning, connection is a practice — one that becomes even more important as we age. The research is clear: strong relationships are one of the most powerful predictors of longevity, resilience, and well-being. But beyond the science, there's the lived experience: life simply feels richer when we share it.

So now that we've explored how to keep your mind expanding, let's turn to the next essential ingredient of aging well — the people who walk the path with you.

Chapter 10 is about the relationships that lift us, the communities that sustain us, and the simple, intentional ways we can build a life filled with connection.

Let's go there next.

CHAPTER 10 — THE LAW OF CONNECTION

The law of connection is simple: Humans are wired to thrive when we are connected to others.

I vividly remember a day more than a decade ago when my loving bride turned to me and said, "I think I want to learn how to shoot a shotgun."

Talk about a comment coming out of left field. Had I done something dreadfully wrong? Should I be concerned for my safety? Where was this coming from?

Turns out, she was serious — she wanted to learn a new skill. But a shotgun?

So I did what any doting husband would do: I went online and found a range offering a "try-it-out" package where a student could spend an hour with a certified instructor learning the history of shotgun sports, the safety basics, and yes — shooting a few targets. I tucked a gift certificate for the class into her Christmas stocking. She was delighted.

Then she dropped the next bombshell: she wanted me to take the lesson with her.

I had never handled a shotgun. I had zero interest in handling a shotgun. But because I love my wife, I agreed.

On a cold, misty Saturday in January, off we went. We were greeted by Chuck, our instructor — a terrific guy who walked us through the fundamentals. Then came the practical part: actually shooting the shotgun.

My wife did great, breaking virtually every clay target thrown. Me? Not so much. I achieved the dubious distinction of being the only "try-it-out" participant not to hit a single target. I imagine I still hold that honor. While I enjoyed watching my bride smile as she pulverized each flying clay, I was pretty happy when the experience was over and we were back in the warm car.

I didn't think about clay target shooting again — until about nine months later, when my lovely bride announced she wanted a shotgun of her own.

A few days later, I drove back to the range for advice. A beautiful Italian-made 20-gauge was ordered, arriving just in time for Christmas — exactly one year after the gift certificate.

Lessons were arranged (for both of us again… why do I let myself get roped into these things?). And this time, something clicked. I learned that just as we have a dominant hand, we also have a dominant eye. I'm right-handed but left-eye dominant, meaning my left eye processes visual information faster. Chuck had me switch to shooting off my left shoulder so my dominant eye could align with the barrel and the target — and suddenly, I started breaking clays. It was fun.

Unfortunately, around the same time, my wife developed a shoulder condition unrelated to shooting, which ended her shooting career. But by then, I was hooked. With her blessing, I kept going. A new hobby was born.

At first, it was a solitary hobby — which suited my introverted nature. I'd go to the range alone, practice what Chuck taught me, and make slow progress. But everything changed when I started meeting other shooters and eventually competing. It was a safe environment for an introvert like me. Over time, I developed friendships that have lasted for years — the kind of friendships where you know you could call someone at midnight and they'd show up to help. We practiced together, helped each other with tough targets, and supported one another even on tournament days when we were technically competitors.

This common interest made making friends easier — something that becomes more challenging as we age.

And as I think about how much this hobby expanded my world, I can't help but think back to my father. When he retired, his social circle collapsed almost overnight. Work had been his only real source of connection, and once it was gone, the friendships that had once been part of his daily life slowly faded. He lived alone, far from family, and without new communities or shared interests to replace what he'd lost. Over time, his world grew smaller and smaller. Looking back now, I can see how isolation accelerated his decline. The research is clear — social isolation and loneliness are linked to poorer physical and mental health, reduced quality of life, and shorter longevity. My father lived that reality. And it's one of the reasons I take connection so seriously today.

When we're young, friendships are handed to us. Our parents arrange playdates. School gives us classmates. College gives us roommates, hallmates, teammates. Early adulthood gives us coworkers and, if we have kids, other parents on the sidelines of soccer fields.

Writers like Arthur Brooks and David Brooks have pointed out how these built-in social structures quietly disappear as we age. And when they do, many of us discover something surprising: for the first time in our lives, we have to work to make new friends — and we're out of practice.

Yet the effort is worth it. Strong social relationships increase our odds of survival by roughly 50%, a benefit comparable to quitting smoking and twice as powerful as regular exercise. Social connection is fundamental to physical, mental, and emotional well-being — hardwired into our neurobiology. High-quality relationships are among the strongest predictors of longevity, rivaling diet, exercise, and genetics.

Connection isn't optional. It's essential.

And sometimes, connection begins with something as simple — and unexpected — as a shotgun lesson on a cold January morning.

Why Connection Matters for Aging Well

Before going deeper, it's worth acknowledging something up front: a few of the themes in this section will echo the opening story. That's intentional. Connection is so essential to healthy aging—and so easy to lose without noticing—that it deserves to be emphasized. We forget this truth not because it's complicated, but because modern life quietly pulls us away from the relationships that sustain us.

Connection is not optional for human beings. It is biological, woven into our nervous system, and essential for healthy aging. For most of human history, survival depended on belonging to a group. Our bodies still operate on that ancient wiring. When we feel connected, our brains release chemicals that calm us, lift our mood, and help us recover from stress. When we feel isolated, our bodies respond as if we're under threat—cortisol rises, inflammation increases, and our health slowly erodes.

The research is clear: loneliness increases the risk of heart disease, stroke, dementia, depression, anxiety, and early mortality. Social isolation is now recognized as a major public health concern. And many of us have seen this play out in real life—a parent, a friend, or even ourselves drifting into isolation as the structures that once held our social world together begin to fade.

Part of the challenge is that connection gets harder as we age. Let me repeat these few sentences as they are important. When we're young, friendships are built into the architecture of our lives. School gives us classmates. College gives us roommates and hallmates. Early adulthood gives us coworkers and, if we have children, other parents on the sidelines of sports fields. We don't have to work very hard to make friends—they're handed to us.

But as life shifts—kids grow up, careers change, routines settle—those built-in social structures disappear. Suddenly, for the first time in our lives, we have to actively make new friends. Many of us discover we're out of practice. Add in introversion, comfort zones, and the ease of staying home, and it becomes even harder.

Yet the effort is worth it. Strong social relationships increase our odds of survival by roughly 50%. Connection is as powerful as quitting smoking and twice as powerful as regular exercise. It is one of the strongest predictors of longevity we have.

Connection doesn't just make us feel good—it makes us better. Emotionally, it gives us belonging and shared joy. Cognitively, conversation stimulates memory, attention, and language. Physically, people with strong social ties move more, eat better, and stick with healthy habits. Identity-wise, connection expands who we are. It keeps us curious, engaged, and open to new experiences.

And in a world where social media offers the illusion of connection without the substance, it's easy to forget how much real human relationships matter. Scrolling through curated snapshots of other people's lives can leave us feeling more isolated, not less. Online interactions lack the richness of shared presence—the body language, tone, laughter, and lived experience that make relationships real.

Connection is a biological necessity. It is emotional nutrition. And it is one of the most powerful tools we have for aging well.

Understanding why connection matters is only half the story. The real challenge—and the real opportunity—is learning how to build it intentionally as we age.

How to Build Connection

If connection is essential, the next question becomes: how do we build it—especially as adults, when it no longer happens automatically? The good news is that connection can be created, strengthened, and rebuilt at any age. It simply requires intention.

Shared interests as the easiest doorway

Shared interests are one of the most reliable ways to form new relationships. A hobby, a sport, a class, a club—these give us something to talk about, something to work on, and something to return to. They remove the awkwardness of "making friends from scratch." Shared activities create shared experiences, and shared experiences create connection. Want a "twofer"? In the last chapter, we talked about the power of lifelong learning. When you sign up for that class at your local college or community center, you might just walk away with a new skill and a new friend.

The workout-buddy effect

Shared physical effort deepens connection in a way few other things do. When you sweat with someone, struggle with someone, and celebrate small victories with someone, the relationship strengthens. It's not just accountability—it's camaraderie. It's shared identity. A workout buddy, a walking partner, a cycling group, a pickleball league—these aren't just fitness tools. They're connection tools.

Remember my reluctance to join my neighbor at the gym? Sure, we knew one another at that point. But now our relationship is on a whole different level because of our shared experiences. We're no longer just neighbors, and not just workout buddies—we're real friends.

Micro-connections as daily social nutrition

Not every connection has to be deep to be meaningful. Micro-connections—those small, positive exchanges we have throughout the day—add warmth and humanity to our lives. A smile at the barista. A wave to another cyclist. A thank-you to a service worker. A quick chat with a neighbor. These tiny moments don't replace deep friendships, but they lift our mood, strengthen our sense of belonging, and keep us socially flexible.

If I had a magic wand and could make one small change in our world, it would be to help people become just a little more friendly with one another. It takes virtually no effort to smile at another human being and acknowledge their existence. And isn't that what we all really crave? To be recognized as a fellow person of value? To be accepted, just as we are? A little kindness, a little acknowledgment—pure and simple. Won't you join me in this effort? And while I am on my soap box, please also take the time to thank those who help you along your journey. We can't do this alone. Friends, and family are the backbone that hold us all up.

Family as a source of lifelong connection

Family is the first community we ever belong to, and often the most enduring. Siblings who shared our childhood, adult children who now see us as peers, grandchildren who bring joy and energy, extended family who carry pieces of our history—these relationships can be some of the richest and most stabilizing connections we have. They require the same ingredients as any other relationship—time, attention, vulnerability, and presence—but the return on investment is enormous.

Since family often ends up spread out geographically, we may have to lean on technology to keep those bonds strong. My wife and I do just that. We have two adult children. One is 1,500 miles away; the other is just a few miles down the road. How do we cope with the distance and two time zones? Constant contact through texting and FaceTime. I've learned to keep pushing buttons on the Apple TV remote until—almost magically—Kris from Colorado appears right there in our living room with us. Staying connected sometimes means becoming more adept with new technologies, which is a double win: it strengthens our relationships and gives our brains a healthy challenge at the same time.

Replacing social media with real connection

Our parish priest once shared a story during his homily—long before social media became what it is today. He told of an older woman who had hundreds of "friends" online. Her posts were liked, her photos were commented on, and her digital world looked full. But when she passed away, not a single person showed up for her funeral. Hundreds of online connections, yet no one physically present to honor her life.

Social media can be a useful tool, but it cannot replace real human interaction. It's easy to confuse scrolling with connecting, but the two are not the same. The goal isn't to abandon social media altogether, but to use it intentionally—as a bridge to real-world interactions, not a substitute for them. And for the record… I don't actually have any social media presence at this time (well maybe Strava – but I consider that a fitness app with some hints at social media). I don't see a need for it in my life. I am often asked how I get so much done in a day… this very well might be the key!

Don't become the woman our priest described. Step away from the keyboard and into real life.

Building deeper friendships

Deep friendships grow through consistency, reciprocity, vulnerability, and shared experiences. They require showing up—not perfectly, but regularly. These are the friendships that sustain us, challenge us, and carry us through the hard seasons of life. They are worth the effort.

Connection doesn't happen by accident. It happens by design—through shared interests, shared effort, small daily interactions, intentional use of technology, and the relationships we choose to nurture. And the beautiful truth is that it's never too late to begin. And it's never too late to improve the friendships we already have.

A year ago, I set out to do just that. In Chapter 12, we'll talk about goal setting, but let me share one goal I set for myself last year: I wanted to become a better friend to the buddies I already had. I chose one simple strategy, inspired by the great Dale Carnegie—to be more interesting, I would become more interested.

What does that look like in practice? It means listening with real intent. Not listening while mentally preparing my response. Not interrupting unnecessarily. Asking questions. Giving the other person space to feel heard and valued.

Did it work? Normally, I'd try to measure the results, but that's a little tricky here. Still, I think it made a difference. At the very least, I felt better after conversations where I practiced this. And it didn't end after my one-year effort. I think I've become a subtly better version of myself. Maybe my friends noticed, maybe they didn't—but it never hurts to try to lift up the people around you.

And just like that first reluctant trip to the shotgun range opened a door I didn't know I needed, every small act of connection has the potential to reshape our lives in ways we can't predict.

Chapter Summary: The Law of Connection

- Connection protects health — lowering stress, inflammation, and risk of chronic disease.
- Isolation increases risk — heart disease, stroke, dementia, depression, and early mortality.
- Connection gets harder with age as built-in social structures fade (school, work, kids' activities).
- Shared interests create easy entry points for new friendships and community.
- Shared physical effort builds camaraderie and deepens relationships through struggle and success.
- Micro-connections matter — small daily interactions lift mood and strengthen belonging.
- Family remains a lifelong anchor — even when distance requires technology to stay close.
- Social media is a tool, not a substitute — real connection happens in real life.
- Deep friendships grow through consistency, reciprocity, and vulnerability.
- Connection is built by design — through intentional actions, not passive hope.

Your Turn

- Identify one shared interest you can pursue with someone this month.
- Choose one relationship to strengthen — family or friend — and take one small action this week.
- Practice one micro-connection each day: a smile, a greeting, a moment of acknowledgment.
- Try the Dale Carnegie approach: be more interested. Listen with intent. Ask questions.
- Replace five minutes of scrolling with a real-world interaction — a text, a call, a visit.
- Take one step toward connection today — however small.

The law of connection is simple: Humans are wired to thrive when we are connected to others.

➤ IT'S NOT WHAT YOU KNOW, IT'S WHAT YOU DO. ➤

PART IV SUMMARY — The Mind

Part IV has been about the mind — the inner world that shapes everything else. Your mindset, your willingness to keep learning, and your ability to build meaningful connection all work together to create a strong, flexible, resilient inner life. When your mind is open, curious, and connected, you move through the world with more confidence and more clarity. You see possibilities where others see limits. You stay engaged, adaptable, and alive.

But even the strongest mind doesn't operate in a vacuum. We live inside a culture that is constantly influencing us — nudging our choices, shaping our expectations, and pulling our attention in a hundred different directions. Some influences help us grow. Others quietly steer us away from the life we want to live.

That's why the next part of this journey stands alone.

Part V is about discernment — learning to recognize the forces around you and choosing which ones deserve a place in your life. It's about filtering the noise, questioning the defaults, and becoming intentional about what you allow to shape your thoughts, habits, and identity.

You've strengthened the mind.

Now it's time to protect it. That's what we will cover in chapter 11.

PART V — INFLUENCES AND CULTURE

You've strengthened your inner world — your mindset, your curiosity, your willingness to keep learning, and your capacity to build meaningful connection. But even the strongest inner life doesn't exist in isolation. Every day, you're surrounded by forces that shape your attention, your expectations, your habits, and your sense of what's possible. Some of those forces lift you up. Others quietly pull you off course.

Part V is about those forces — the cultural currents, social pressures, digital inputs, and environmental cues that influence how you think, how you feel, and how you age. You don't control all of them. But you do control which ones you allow into your life.

This part of the book is about discernment: the ability to recognize what serves you and what doesn't. It's about filtering the noise, questioning the defaults, and choosing your influences with intention. Because the world is always shaping you — the only question is whether it's shaping you by accident or by design.

Chapter 11 introduces the Law of Discernment, the principle that helps you protect your mind, your time, your energy, and your identity. It's the final external law before we move into the last part of the book — the part where everything comes together and you learn how to live this system with clarity, consistency, and joy.

CHAPTER 11 — THE LAW OF DISCERNMENT

The law of discernment is simple: You become what you allow into your life — choose your inputs with intention.

You may imagine that your daily choices work like a cafeteria line: everything laid out neatly, portioned sensibly, organized so you can make thoughtful decisions. But modern life isn't a cafeteria — it's an all-you-can-eat buffet. Endless options, oversized portions, and everything engineered to make you take more than you need. And if we're being honest, it's not even a buffet anymore. It's a firehose. Information, opinions, outrage, entertainment, advertising, and noise blasting at you from every direction, all day long. Discernment is the skill that lets you step out of the spray, choose what actually belongs on your plate, and design a life that supports who you want to become.

When you live in a world like this, discernment stops being optional. It becomes a daily practice. You can't control the buffet. You can't turn off the firehose. But you can decide what you put on your plate. You can choose the inputs that nourish you and ignore the ones that drain you. That's the heart of this chapter. The law of discernment is simple: you become what you consume. Your influences shape your beliefs, your habits, your identity, and ultimately your future. If you want to be ageless by design, you have to choose your inputs with intention.

Let me give you a simple example of how this plays out in real life. Years ago, I owned a BlackBerry Storm 2 — a device famous for one thing: a tiny blinking red light that signaled a new message. That little light was the perfect symbol of the buffet-and-firehose world we live in. It didn't matter what I was doing — eating dinner, talking with my wife, reading a book — if that light blinked, it hijacked my attention. I wasn't choosing my inputs. They were choosing me.

Eventually, I realized how much control I had given away. So I made a change. My phone no longer enters the bedroom. It stays downstairs at night. All notifications are turned off. The volume on my computer is muted. I decide when I check messages, not the other way around.

This is discernment in its simplest form: limiting the firehose, shrinking the buffet, and choosing what gets onto your mental plate. Multitasking is a myth. Every time we shift our attention, our brain has to reset. We don't get more done — we just do more things poorly.

Discernment starts with attention. If you don't control your inputs, your inputs will control you.

Discernment starts with attention, but it doesn't end there. The same principle applies to everything you allow into your life — the news you follow, the conversations you engage in, the people you spend time with, the environments you choose, even the beliefs you absorb without realizing it. In a world built like a buffet and delivered like a firehose, the default is to take in far more than you need and far more than is good for you. Discernment is the skill that lets you pause, step back, and ask a simple question: Does this belong on my plate? When you begin choosing your inputs with intention, you start shaping your identity with intention. And that's the foundation of an ageless life by design.

Let me confess something: I used to be a news "junkie." My day started with *my* morning newspaper at breakfast — and I emphasize "my" because no one else was allowed to touch it until I had first crack at it. Not my finest quality, but it shows how serious I was about staying informed. I read the paper cover to cover every single day.

That was just the beginning. I watched the evening news at 6:00. I checked cable news throughout the day. I refreshed internet feeds constantly. And when I got in the car, satellite radio offered me an entire buffet of 24/7 news channels. No matter where I was or what I was doing, I could mainline news on demand.

Was I informed? Absolutely. But I wasn't just informed — I was inundated. There's nothing wrong with knowing what's happening in the world. We don't want to be ostriches with our heads in the sand. But just like weighing yourself daily — something I still consider useful — there's a point of diminishing returns. And beyond that point, the returns turn negative. Checking the news all day becomes an obsession, a compulsion, an anxiety machine fueled by constant outrage just as weighing yourself – say 5 times per day would only elevate anxiety.

Then a few bellwether events happened in print media. You probably noticed the same thing. Prices went up. Actual content went down. My daily newspaper kept shrinking. During my early morning dog walks, I saw fewer and fewer papers on driveways. My neighbors were dropping subscriptions left and right. Eventually, I was the last holdout — and even I finally canceled.

At first, I missed it. The newspaper offered me a digital subscription, but Pandora's box had already been opened. I started asking myself a simple question: What decisions am I actually making based on what I read every day? I couldn't think of a single one — unless you count which grocery store had the best deal on Cheerios.

That realization spread. I asked the same question about all the news sources I consumed around the clock. The answer was the same. My "need to stay informed" was really just a voyeuristic habit dressed up as responsibility. It wasn't serving me. It wasn't improving my life. It wasn't helping me make better decisions. It was just noise.

So I started cutting off the news sources one by one. And you know what happened? Nothing. Nothing in my life changed. The world kept spinning. I didn't miss anything important. What I kept was minimal — just enough to stay aware of major events locally and globally. And that turned out to be surprisingly easy. A local TV station had an app with clean summaries of local, state, national, and international news. I could catch up in one or two minutes a day. No drama. No outrage. No firehose.

I was informed — but no longer inundated. News, as I had known it, was no longer allowed on my plate.

What I gained was time. And with that time, something more important happened: my identity shifted. I stopped being a reactive consumer of media and became a deliberate one. I replaced the illusion of "staying up to date" with a more intentional practice. I read more books. I chose what I wanted to allow into my mind. I filled my attention with things that actually improved my life, helped me make better decisions, and dramatically lowered my anxiety.

That's the power of discernment.

Stepping away from the firehose didn't leave me uninformed — it left me with space. And in that space, something important happened: I became far more intentional about who I listened to and what I allowed onto my mental plate. Instead of reacting to whatever the buffet shoved in front of me, I started curating my inputs the way you would in a well-designed cafeteria: a few high-quality choices, clearly labeled, portioned sensibly, and aligned with the life I wanted to build. Books, long-form thinkers, trusted voices, and carefully chosen feeds began replacing the noise. I wasn't consuming less information — I was consuming better information. And that shift didn't just change what I knew; it changed what I did, how I felt, and who I was becoming.

Who I Listen to and How I Choose

So I read. And I read. And I read. I could fill chapters with the hundreds of books I've consumed over the years, but a few authors have had an outsized influence on how I think and how I live. David Brooks and Arthur C. Brooks on purpose. Mark Hyman and Gabrielle Lyon on functional medicine and longevity. Ryan Holiday on the stoic way. The Gottmans on relationships. Angela Duckworth on grit. Darrin Donnelly on mindset and applied psychology. Jonathan Haidt and Mo Gawdat on happiness. Carol Dweck on mindset. Daniel Lieberman on exercise. Mihaly Csikszentmihalyi on flow. I could keep going, but that list alone makes a pretty good checklist.

And I didn't stop with print. I became just as selective about who I allowed into my head through my earphones. Steven Bartlett's *Diary of a CEO* podcast — and his book by the same name — consistently brings thoughtful, high-quality guests. Andrew Huberman's podcast offers deep dives into physiology, behavior, and performance. These became part of my curated input stream.

But here's the key word: "Consideration".

I read and listen widely, but I don't accept anything blindly. This is where the cafeteria analogy comes back into play. I walk the line, I look at what's offered, and I choose what goes on my plate. Even within a single source, I pick and choose what works for me.

Take Bryan Johnson, for example. His "Blueprint" project is one of the most ambitious longevity experiments ever attempted. He spends millions of dollars a year testing protocols on himself. Do I want his lifestyle? Not even close. But I've learned from him. My own structured meal planning was inspired by studying his work — though he'd probably choke if he saw what my version actually looks like. The point is simple: learn from what others are doing, but decide what works for you.

Another example: creatine. You may remember my experiment from earlier in the book. You can find a new article every day praising its benefits. But when I tried it, my HRV dropped — and that was a trade-off I wasn't willing to make at the time. Does that mean I'll never take creatine? No. I'll keep an eye on the science with an open mind. The same goes for the multivitamin I kicked off my plate. I don't accept dogma, but I don't ignore new developments either.

Discernment also applies to exercise. Search the internet for "how to do a pull-up" and prepare to spend the rest of your afternoon reading. Thousands of resources. Hundreds of variations. I'm not interested in finding the one true optimal pull-up. It's a basic exercise. A local trainer can teach you in under five minutes. The basics will serve you well. That doesn't mean I ignore all the workout videos online — but I've found one or two voices I trust and I stick with them.

One of the most helpful came from my wife. She introduced me to Will Tennyson, a Canadian bodybuilder and fitness influencer. His advice on chest and shoulder development has been invaluable in shaping my current workout plan. As with everything else, I keep my training simple and structured, and I only change it when I find something better than what I'm currently doing. Will's guidance met that bar. (Fair warning: he's funny, but he does use some colorful language and crass innuendo. Sensitive ears beware.)

The pattern here is simple: curate, don't copy.

Consider, don't consume blindly.

Choose, don't default.

Discernment isn't about limiting your world — it's about designing it.

Discernment and Friendships

Doing this with news, books, and internet advice is one thing. But what about when discernment requires us to rethink — or even release — certain friendships? That's harder. But it's just as important.

It's a slight modification of the cafeteria analogy:

Who do you allow to sit with you and accompany you on your life's journey?

Before we get to real-world friendships, let's revisit social media. As I mentioned in the last chapter, I don't currently have a social media presence of any kind. I know I'm the exception.

So instead of offering advice from experience, I'll offer a few questions worth considering:

- How much time are you spending each day on social media?
- Is it positively contributing to your life or your decisions?
- What's the actual value?
- How much of it is voyeuristic — titillation disguised as connection?
- Do you fall into the "compare and despair" trap?
- Do you check to see how many likes you're getting?
- Are your social media "friends" truly your friends?
- How would you feel if you couldn't access social media for a day… a week… a month… or permanently?
- Are you practicing cafeteria, buffet, or firehose principles with your social media involvement?

These are tough questions. But now apply them to your real-world friendships.

My wife has a favorite saying:

"Friends can be for a reason, a season, or a lifetime."

Sometimes we need to ask the hard questions about our friendships — especially when they're no longer workable or contributing in a positive way.

I've had to do this a few times in my life. One friend's ethics no longer aligned with my values. Another was continuously emotionally draining. The first was easier to let go of. The second was harder. I want to be a good friend to those who need me — but not at the expense of my own mental health.

Sometimes:

- The reason for a friendship no longer exists.
- The season has come to an end.
- And some friendships that feel "lifelong" are actually masquerading as something they're not.

Just as we prune trees to help them grow beautifully, we sometimes need to prune our friendships to allow our own lives to grow beautifully. It's one of the more challenging parts of discernment — but also one of the most necessary.

Discernment in friendships is never easy, but it's essential. The people we allow into our lives shape our beliefs, our habits, our emotional landscape, and even our sense of what's possible. Inputs aren't just digital — they're human. And just as we curate what we read, watch, and listen to, we also have to curate the relationships that surround us. This isn't about judgment or superiority; it's about alignment, health, and growth. When you choose who sits at your table, you're choosing the environment you live in — and environment, as we'll explore next, is one of the most powerful predictors of happiness and well-being. Discernment isn't just about what you consume. It's about the world you build around yourself.

Discernment and Your Environment

Discernment doesn't stop with information, influences, or friendships. It extends to something even more fundamental: the environment you choose to live in.

I have fond memories of the first house Ann and I lived in after we got married. It was a lovely townhouse in a great town. It's where we learned how to navigate married life. We had wonderful neighbors. It was home. But it had drawbacks. We lived in the end unit closest to a main road. Our bedroom and deck faced the traffic. It wasn't a highway, but the noise was constant — whether we were trying to enjoy the deck or sleep. And being at the end of the building meant parking was a daily frustration. Spots were often taken, and the layout made getting in and out a challenge.

Contrast that with our current home, where we've lived for more than twenty-five years. It's in a quiet residential neighborhood. I have an app on my phone that identifies birds by their calls. When I step onto our deck — which, thankfully, doesn't face the road — the app usually picks up ten different species within moments. It's peaceful. It's restorative. We have easy access to the greenway system for walks and bike rides. We have our own garage. No parking battles. Every time my mother-in-law visited, she would say, "This is like living in a park." And she was right.

Which environment is more conducive to joy? It's not even close.

And there's science behind that intuition. In his fantastic book *The Happiness Hypothesis*, Jonathan Haidt describes an equation for happiness in which one of the key variables is C — control. The environment you choose to live in is one of the most powerful ways to increase the amount of control you actually have. I first read Haidt's book in 2015, and his insight about shaping your environment has stayed with me ever since.

So consider your own environment. Are there things you can control that would make it more peaceful? Is this an area where an investment — of time, money, or attention — might pay dividends in your happiness? Could you make better decisions, or simply feel more grounded, if your surroundings supported you instead of draining you?

I'm not suggesting we run away from our problems by changing our address. But I am saying this: where you live affects how you live. Your environment absolutely influences your capacity to experience happiness.

What I learned from those two homes is something Jonathan Haidt put into words far better than I ever could: your environment isn't just where you live — it's one of the strongest forces shaping how you feel. In *The Happiness Hypothesis*, Haidt argues that happiness isn't simply a matter of willpower or mindset. It's deeply influenced by the conditions around us — the noise, the beauty, the safety, the friction, the ease, the daily cues that either lift us up or wear us down. His "C" for control isn't about controlling everything in life; it's about designing the parts you can control so they support your well-being instead of undermining it. When you change your environment, you change the baseline from which your emotions operate. You change the default. You change the starting point. And that's one of the most powerful forms of discernment there is.

Environment as a Predictor of Happiness

Jonathan Haidt's work helped me see something I had felt intuitively for years: happiness isn't just an inside job. It's also an outside job. We tend to think of happiness as something we generate through mindset, discipline, or sheer willpower. But Haidt argues that a huge portion of our emotional life is shaped by the environment we place ourselves in — the sights, sounds, rhythms, stresses, and supports that surround us every day.

In other words, your environment is not neutral. It's either lifting you up or wearing you down.

Haidt uses the metaphor of the rider and the elephant — the conscious mind and the emotional mind. The rider can try to steer, but the elephant is powerful. And one of the best ways to influence the elephant isn't through force or motivation, but through changing the path. Change the environment, and the elephant naturally moves in a different direction.

That idea changed how I thought about my own life. It helped me understand why our second home felt so different from our first. It wasn't just quieter. It wasn't just prettier. It wasn't just more convenient. It was an environment that supported calm, clarity, and better decisions. It was a place where the "path" made it easier to live the life I wanted to live.

And that's the heart of discernment:

Design the path so your best choices become your easiest choices.

When your environment supports you, you don't have to fight yourself all day. You don't have to rely on willpower. You don't have to swim upstream. You simply live in a space that nudges you toward better habits, better moods, and better decisions.

So ask yourself:

- Does your environment make it easier or harder to be the person you want to be?
- Does it calm you or agitate you?
- Does it support your routines or sabotage them?
- Does it give you space to think, rest, and recover?
- Does it help you show up as your best self?

These aren't small questions. They're foundational. Because when you change your environment — even in small ways — you change the emotional baseline from which your entire life operates.

Discernment isn't just about choosing what goes on your plate. It's about choosing the kitchen, the table, the room, and the view. It's about designing the world around you so it supports the world within you.

Designing an Environment That Supports You

If environment is one of the strongest predictors of happiness, then shaping your environment becomes one of the most powerful forms of discernment. The goal isn't perfection. It's alignment. You want to create surroundings that make it easier to live the life you want — not harder.

And the good news is that you don't need to move houses to do this. You can start with small, intentional changes that shift the emotional tone of your daily life.

Here are a few places to begin:

1. Reduce friction for the habits you want

- If you want to walk more, make your walking shoes the easiest thing to grab.
- If you want to read more, keep a book on the table where you drink your morning coffee.
- If you want to stretch in the evenings, leave a yoga mat out where you can see it.

Small environmental cues can make a big difference. They lower the activation energy required to do the things you already want to do.

2. Increase friction for the habits you don't want

This is the flip side of the same principle.

- If you want to watch less TV, unplug it or keep the remote in another room.
- If you want to check your phone less, charge it outside the bedroom.

- If you want to snack less, don't keep the snacks in the house.

You're not relying on willpower — you're designing the path.

3. Create pockets of calm

Your environment should include at least one place where your nervous system can exhale.

- A quiet reading chair.
- A clean desk.
- A peaceful corner of the backyard.
- A room where the lighting is soft and the noise is low.

These small sanctuaries matter more than we realize.

4. Surround yourself with signals of who you want to become. This is one of the most underrated forms of environmental design.

- A bookshelf filled with the thinkers who inspire you.
- A journal on your nightstand.
- A bike in the garage that's ready to ride.
- A kitchen organized around the meals you want to cook.
- A calendar that reflects your values, not your obligations.

Your environment should whisper your identity back to you.

5. Remove the things that drain you. Sometimes the most powerful environmental change is subtraction.

- Clutter.
- Noise.
- Toxic reminders.
- Old projects that weigh on you.
- Spaces that feel chaotic or overwhelming.

Removing these isn't cosmetic — it's psychological. It frees up mental bandwidth and emotional space.

6. Add beauty where you can. Beauty is not a luxury. It's nourishment.

- A plant.
- A piece of art.
- A candle.
- A photograph that makes you smile.
- A view of trees instead of a screen.

Beauty changes how you feel in a space, and how you feel in a space changes how you live in it.

The Principle Behind It All

The deeper truth is this: Your environment is always shaping you — the only question is whether it's doing so by default or by design.

Discernment means choosing the design.

When you intentionally shape your surroundings, you're not just improving your home or your workspace. You're improving your emotional baseline. You're making it easier to be calm, focused, healthy, and joyful. You're creating a life where your best choices become your natural choices.

And that's the essence of being ageless by design.

Discernment and Your Beliefs

It's one thing to curate your news, your influences, your friendships, and your environment. But what about the deepest layer of all — your beliefs? Changing your physical surroundings is relatively easy. Changing the internal architecture of your mind is something else entirely.

It's commonly accepted that what we believe shapes what we value, and what we value shapes our actions and habits. But that raises an uncomfortable question: How did we form those beliefs in the first place? And more importantly, are they still serving us?

Warren Buffett has famously said, "The highest form of intelligence is to change your mind when the facts change." His longtime business partner, Charlie Munger, took this even further with what he called his "Best Loved Ideas Rule." Each year, he would deliberately seek out one long-held belief that no longer served him — and replace it. Not because it was easy, but because it was necessary.

And let's be honest: this is not easy to do. In fact, it's getting harder.

With social media and AI-curated feeds, we're increasingly surrounded by information that reinforces what we already believe. You've probably noticed this yourself — your feeds keep showing you more of what you "like," and less of anything that challenges your viewpoint. This funnel effect makes us more susceptible to confirmation bias. We don't even have to go looking for evidence that supports our beliefs; technology delivers it to us automatically.

Discernment means resisting that drift. It means making decisions that serve us — and having the courage to change those decisions when the facts change. But it takes effort. It takes humility. And it takes a willingness to sit with discomfort.

Buffett has another practice that illustrates this beautifully: he refuses to make a decision until he understands the counterarguments at least as well as the people making them. That is discernment in action — not just knowing your position, but knowing the strongest version of the opposing one.

So how do we practice that in our own lives?

Recently, my wife and I were having a political discussion. We were on the same side of the issue, but there was a high-profile political figure who took the opposing position to an extreme. It would have been easy to attack her or dismiss her entirely. But we had to admit — reluctantly — that while we didn't agree with her conclusions, we could appreciate her willingness to question assumptions we ourselves held. That wasn't a comfortable realization. We didn't want to give any credit to the opposing viewpoint. But the truth was there.

Seeing the good in alternative views doesn't mean abandoning your own. It simply means allowing those views a little air time in your consciousness. It means acknowledging that you might not have the full picture. And who knows — you might even change your mind.

That's the heart of discernment:

the willingness to examine your beliefs with honesty, humility, and courage — and to update them when reality demands it.

Discernment is not a single skill — it's a way of moving through the world. It's the quiet, steady practice of choosing what you allow into your mind, your relationships, your environment, and your belief system. It's the art of designing a life that supports who you want to become rather than letting the world decide for you. When you step back from the firehose, shrink the buffet, and choose what belongs on your plate, you reclaim something precious: the ability to live with intention. Discernment doesn't make life easier, but it makes life clearer. And clarity is the foundation of an ageless life by design.

Chapter Summary: The Law of Discernment

Your attention is your most valuable resource; discernment begins with choosing your inputs.

- Information is abundant, but wisdom requires filtering — not everything deserves space on your plate.
- Curating your influences (books, podcasts, experts) helps shape your identity with intention.
- Discernment applies to relationships too — some friendships are for a reason, a season, or a lifetime.
- Your environment is a powerful predictor of happiness; design it to support your well-being.
- Your internal environment — your beliefs — may require the most courage to examine and update.
- Confirmation bias and curated feeds make belief-discernment harder, but also more essential.
- True discernment includes understanding opposing viewpoints as well as your own.

When you choose your inputs, you shape your identity. When you shape your identity, you shape your future.

Your Turn

- Identify one area of your life where the "firehose" is still running — news, social media, email, or something else. Reduce the flow.
- Choose one influence (a book, a thinker, a podcast) that consistently elevates you — and one that no longer deserves space.
- Evaluate a friendship through the lens of "reason, season, or lifetime." What category does it truly belong in?
- Make one small environmental change that increases peace or reduces friction in your daily routine.
- Examine one belief you've held for years. Ask yourself whether it still serves you — and whether the facts have changed.

The law of discernment is simple: You become what you allow into your life — choose your inputs with intention.

➤ IT'S NOT WHAT YOU KNOW, IT'S WHAT YOU DO. ➤

PART V SUMMARY — Influences and Culture

Part V has been about the forces that shape us — the inputs we consume, the people we surround ourselves with, the environments we inhabit, and the beliefs we carry. These influences matter because they quietly sculpt our identity and guide our choices, often without our awareness. Discernment gives us the tools to choose those influences with intention rather than drift.

But understanding your influences is only part of the journey. The next step — the final step — is integration. It's where everything you've learned throughout this book comes together into a cohesive, sustainable system. Because a well-designed life isn't built on isolated habits or one-off insights. It's built on systems that support your identity, reinforce your values, and make your best choices the natural ones.

Part VI is about creating that system — the architecture that holds your life together and keeps you aligned with the person you are becoming. This is where design becomes destiny.

PART VI — Integration

You've learned the laws that shape a long, healthy, intentional life — the laws of purpose, daily practice, measurement, mindset, learning, connection, and discernment. Each one has given you a new way to understand yourself and a new tool to shape your future. But knowledge alone doesn't create change. Integration does.

Part VI is about bringing everything together — turning individual insights into a cohesive system that supports you every day, in every season of life. Because aging well isn't about doing everything perfectly. It's about designing a life that makes the right things easier, the meaningful things automatic, and the joyful things unavoidable.

This final part of the book introduces the two laws that hold the entire framework together: the Law of Systems and the Law of Joy. Systems give your life structure. Joy gives your life energy. Together, they create a way of living that is sustainable, resilient, and deeply human.

You've built the foundation. You've strengthened the mind. You've learned to choose your influences with intention. Now it's time to build the life that lasts — and the life that feels good to live.

CHAPTER 12: THE LAW OF SYSTEMS

The Law of Systems Is Simple: Design the structure that supports who you're becoming.

You've spent the last eleven chapters learning how to design an ageless life—one belief, one habit, one relationship, one environment at a time. But now we arrive at the moment where the rubber truly hits the road. This is where everything you've learned stops being theory and becomes a system. A system that supports your identity, reinforces your values, and makes your best choices the natural ones. You don't build an intentional life by accident. You build it by assembling the pieces—your strengths, your gaps, your goals, your routines—into a structure that works for you. This chapter is about creating that structure. It's about integration. It's about designing the engine that will carry you forward for the rest of your life.

And to build that engine, we're going to walk through a six-step process — a blueprint you can personalize and return to for the rest of your life.

You bought this book expecting to learn my 13 laws for intentional living — and I hope I've delivered on that promise. I never offered quick hacks or magic pills. What I did promise was a blueprint, one built from the lived experience of the fifteen years since losing my father. In a way, that is a hack: you get to shortcut a decade and a half of trial, error, reading, reflection, and growth into a process that may take you only a few weeks or months.

But here's the truth: it still takes work. It takes introspection, thinking, experimenting, and a willingness to be honest with yourself. The six-step program that follows is your roadmap for building your own personal blueprint — the one that will guide the rest of your life.

Here is the roadmap of the six steps so you can see what is coming your way:

Step One — Conduct a Gap Analysis
Step Two — Formalize a New Self-Image
Step Three — Develop Clear Objectives
Step Four — Build the Habits That Bring Your Identity to Life
Step Five — Build the Systems That Support Your Life
Step Six — Bring It All Together

We'll repeat this roadmap at the start of each step so you can easily see where you are on the journey.

Step One — Conduct a Gap Analysis

This step is crucial, but it's not difficult. In fact, I've already given you everything you need. I'd like to invite you to pause and take inventory of where you currently stand with each of the eleven laws we've covered so far.

How do you do that?

Start with the "Your Turn" section at the end of each chapter. Each one is a diagnostic tool. Together, they form a personal audit. Work through each of those sections slowly and honestly.

As you do, look for:

- Patterns
- Blind spots
- Strengths
- Areas of friction
- Opportunities for growth

A powerful way to approach this is by performing a personal SWOT analysis. It may sound like something from a corporate boardroom, but it's just as effective at the individual level:

Strengths: What's already working?

Weaknesses: What consistently trips you up?

Opportunities: What could you build on?

Threats: What undermines your progress?

This isn't about judgment. It's about clarity.

A system can only be built on truth.

Write your thoughts down. You don't need to formalize action plans yet — that comes soon. For now, capture what you see, feel, and think. Even better, share your observations with a close friend or spouse. Ask them whether they see the same things from the outside looking in.

And please — don't just think about doing this step. Reading about it won't get it done. You have to do the work. Remember: ***it's not what you know, it's what you do***. Now is the time for the ***doing***.

Don't rush this exercise. This is a long game. It may take time for things to gel. It took me fifteen years. You can easily work through two or three chapters a week — but the key is to actually do it.

And don't feel like anything you write is set in stone. This is your blueprint. You can revise it anytime. In fact, I'd be disappointed if you didn't.

Step One — Conduct a Gap Analysis
Step Two — Formalize a New Self-Image
Step Three — Develop Clear Objectives
Step Four — Build the Habits That Bring Your Identity to Life
Step Five — Build the Systems That Support Your Life
Step Six — Bring It All Together

Once you have your thoughts down on paper in a way that makes sense to you, you're ready to move on to Step Two. And guess what — you already have the tools for this step too.

Identity is the foundation of every system. I hope you've been thinking about your own identity ever since you read Chapter 8. I'm willing to bet the Step One exercise you just completed got you reflecting more deeply on who you want to become for the rest of your life. Now it's time to articulate that vision more clearly — and in writing. Keep your Step One notes close as you work on this step.

Before you begin, I'd like to invite you to go back and reread Chapter 8 in its entirety to "set the mood." As you read, be thinking about:

- your values
- your aspirations
- your lived experience
- your desired future

This is the emotional engine of your system.

Once you've revisited Chapter 8, craft your new self-image statement. Take your time. Share it with someone you trust if that helps you clarify your thinking. And be sure to write it in the present tense — as though you are already living this new identity. Because this is the new person you are becoming.

A strong self-image pulls behavior upward, and that's exactly where you're headed.

And don't worry about perfection. This is not part of your "permanent record." You can revise it as you grow and as life changes — not to escape reality, but to embrace it. Your self-image should evolve as you evolve. That's the whole point of intentional living.

Now that you've articulated your new self-image — the person you are becoming — it's time to give that identity something to stand on. Identity is the emotional engine, but engines need direction. They need structure. They need a path to follow. That's where objectives come in.

Your self-image tells you who you are.

Your objectives tell you what that person does.

This next step is where your vision becomes concrete. It's where you translate identity into action, and action into momentum. And don't worry — just like the first two steps, you already have most of the raw materials you need to do this one. You've been practicing pieces of it throughout the book. Now we're going to assemble them into a clear, practical framework you can use for the rest of your life.

Step One — Conduct a Gap Analysis
Step Two — Formalize a New Self-Image
Step Three — Develop Clear Objectives
Step Four — Build the Habits That Bring Your Identity to Life
Step Five — Build the Systems That Support Your Life
Step Six — Bring It All Together

Now that you've clarified your identity and written your self-image statement, it's time to give that identity direction. Objectives are where your vision becomes concrete. They translate who you are becoming into what that person does.

But before we go any further, let me reassure you of something important:

You do NOT need to create goals for all eleven laws right now.

This is a long game. You build an intentional life the same way you eat an elephant — one bite at a time. Start with one or two areas that matter most today. Momentum will take care of the rest.

With that in mind, let's build your objectives.

The Three Types of Goals

Sport psychology gives us a simple, powerful framework for setting goals. Even though it comes from athletics, it applies beautifully to everyday life.

1. Process Goals

These focus on how you will do something — the behaviors, strategies, and techniques you practice.

They are fully within your control.

Examples:

- Practicing mindful eating at one meal per day
- Strength training twice a week
- Setting aside 10 minutes each morning for reflection
- Using active listening during conversations with your spouse
- Preparing healthy lunches on Sundays

Process goals build identity through repetition.

2. Performance Goals

These measure improvement relative to your past performance.

They show progress — and progress builds confidence.

Examples:

- Increasing weekly steps from 40,000 to 60,000
- Improving average sleep from 6.5 to 7.5 hours
- Reducing resting heart rate by 3–5 bpm
- Initiating more meaningful conversations each week
- Improving meal-planning consistency from 2 days to 5

Performance goals help you see that your efforts are working.

3. Outcome Goals

These focus on the end result — the "win."

They're influenced by factors outside your control.

Examples:

- Losing 10 pounds by summer
- Completing a 5K this year
- Reaching a target body-fat percentage
- Saving a specific amount of money
- Repairing a strained relationship

Outcome goals give direction, but they shouldn't carry your emotional weight.

Most people overload their lives with outcome goals — the finish lines, the big wins, the "I want to lose 20 pounds" or "I want to run a 5K" declarations. The problem is that outcome goals are the least controllable part of the process. They depend on timing, circumstances, and sometimes luck. A better balance looks like this: about 60% process goals, 30% performance goals, and 10% outcome goals. Process goals build your habits. Performance goals show your progress. Outcome goals give you direction. When you blend them, you stop chasing results and start building the system that produces them.

What Makes a Goal Effective?

Effective goals share several characteristics:

- **S**pecific — clearly defined
- **M**easurable — you know when you've achieved them
- **A**chievable — within your current capabilities
- **R**ealistic — challenging but not punishing
- **T**ime-bound — anchored to a date
- Written down — clarity increases commitment
- Positively framed — focused on what you will do
- Supported by a strategy — not just intention
- A mix of short- and long-term — to build momentum

The SMART acronym is a helpful memory tool, but the real power comes from alignment with your identity. Before you lock in any goal, pause and revisit your why. A goal without a why is just a task; a goal with a why becomes a commitment.

If You're Out of Practice Setting Goals…

If it's been a while since you've set goals, or if this whole section feels a little uncomfortable, here are a few simple tips to help you get started:

- Start with one identity statement. Pick the part of you that feels most important right now.
- Choose one small process goal that expresses it. Make it something you can actually do this week.
- Add one performance goal to measure progress. Just enough to see improvement, not perfection.
- Keep the outcome goal light. It's the direction, not the pressure.
- Revisit your why. A strong why turns effort into meaning.
- Keep it simple. If a goal feels heavy, shrink it until it feels doable.

This isn't about designing the perfect plan; it's about taking the next honest step toward the person you're becoming.

A Final Few Words Before You Begin

Your objectives are not a contract. They're not a test. They're not a measure of your worth. They are tools — tools that help you live as the person you've chosen to become. Start small. Start honest. Start with one bite. The system will grow with you.

The point isn't to design the perfect goal, it's to create goals you can actually do.

You've just done something most people skip — you created clear, honest objectives that align with who you're becoming. That's no small thing. Most readers never make it this far, and you should feel good about the work you've done here.

Now it's time for the part that brings everything to life.

Objectives give you direction, but habits and routines are what turn direction into daily reality. This next step is where your goals stop living on the page and start living in your day. It's where identity becomes action, and action becomes your new normal.

Welcome to Step Four — the part where we build the system that carries you forward.

Step One — Conduct a Gap Analysis
Step Two — Formalize a New Self-Image
Step Three — Develop Clear Objectives
Step Four — Build the Habits That Bring Your Identity to Life
Step Five — Build the Systems That Support Your Life
Step Six — Bring It All Together

You've set your direction. Now it's time to build the rhythms that make that direction real.

Habits are where identity becomes visible. They're the small, repeatable actions that quietly shape who you become. And the good news is that you don't need dozens of them — just a few that matter.

Let me show you what this looks like in my own life.

I start my mornings with a simple routine: I head downstairs, pet our German Shepherd Tessa (95% of the time she sleeps downstairs, 5% of the time she sneaks into bed with us in the early hours), prepare Ann's coffee, check my Fitbit data, triage my work requirements for the day, and lace up my walking shoes for a 30-minute walk with Tessa.

It's not dramatic. It's quiet. It's peaceful. No doom scrolling. No news checking. Just movement, reflection, and intention. This habit anchors my day and supports the identity I'm choosing — someone who moves, someone who reflects, someone who starts the day intentionally.

Even preparing Ann's coffee is a tiny way to express love and appreciation — reinforcing my goal to nurture our connection.

Most of my habits look like that: small, obvious, easy to repeat. That's the secret. Good habits don't require willpower; they require design. When a habit is simple, visible, and rewarding, it becomes part of your life almost without effort.

That's what we're going to build here.

The Intention You Don't Realize You Have

The other day I had lunch with an 84-year-old friend who's in remarkable shape — strong, sharp, steady. He's been following the progress of this book, so I was explaining the idea of intentional living and how habits express identity. He listened, nodded, and finally said, "I get what you're saying… but I don't think I've been intentional about any of this."

But the more we talked, the clearer it became that he has been intentional — just not in the way he labels it.

He golfs every week. He walks the course instead of riding, even when the rest of his foursome hops in a cart. He pays attention to how he feels. He moves his body. He stays engaged. None of it is dramatic. None of it is written down. But it's all intentional.

He made a choice — quietly, consistently — to walk.

And that choice has shaped his fitness, his blood pressure, his energy, and his quality of life.

He didn't call it intention.

But that's exactly what it was.

Most of us are already doing things like this. We just haven't taken the time to notice them, name them, or appreciate them. When you pause and look closely at your own life, you'll see small habits that are already working in your favor. And once you see them, you can build on them — using the same approach to support your other goals.

What You're Already Doing Counts

Before you design new habits, take a moment to notice the ones you already have. Most people underestimate themselves here. They assume intention has to look formal — written goals, color-coded calendars, perfectly structured routines.

But intention often shows up quietly.

You might already be doing things that support your health, your relationships, your mindset, or your sense of purpose — you just haven't named them yet. And once you do name them, you can build on them with confidence instead of starting from scratch.

Here's a simple way to uncover the habits that are already working in your favor.

A Quick Reflection: What Are You Already Doing Well?

Take a moment and scan your day, your week, or your month. Look for small actions that reflect the person you want to be — even if you've never thought of them as "habits" before.

Use these prompts to guide you:

- Movement: When do you naturally choose to move your body? (Walking the dog, taking the stairs, stretching in the morning.)
- Health: What choices do you make without thinking that support your well-being? (Drinking water, cooking at home, going to bed at a consistent time.)
- Connection: How do you show up for the people you care about? (Checking in on a friend, making coffee for your partner, sending a quick text.)

- Learning or curiosity: What do you gravitate toward when you have a few minutes? (Reading, listening to a podcast, practicing a hobby.)
- Purpose or contribution: Where do you naturally invest your energy? (Helping someone, volunteering, mentoring, creating.)

You don't need to force anything here. Just notice.

Awareness is the first step toward intentional design.

Why This Matters

When you recognize the habits you already have, three things happen:

- You build confidence. You're not starting from zero — you're building from strength.
- You see your identity more clearly. Your actions reveal who you already are.
- You create a foundation for new habits. It's easier to add a new rhythm when you understand the ones that already exist.

This is the bridge between where you are and where you're going.

Connecting Your Existing Habits Back to Steps 1–3

By now, you've uncovered a few habits you're already doing well — the quiet, consistent actions that support your health, your relationships, your curiosity, or your sense of purpose. And here's the important part:

These habits didn't come out of nowhere.

They're connected to the work you've already done in this chapter.

In Step One, you identified the gap between where you are and where you want to be.

In Step Two, you clarified the identity you're growing into.

In Step Three, you set objectives that align with that identity.

Now, when you look at the habits you're already practicing, you'll start to see something surprising:

You've been living pieces of that identity all along.

You just didn't call it intention.

My 84-year-old friend didn't think he was being intentional either. But his choice to walk the golf course every week — when everyone else rides — is a perfect example of identity in action. He didn't label it as a "habit" or a "goal." He simply made a choice that aligned with the kind of person he wanted to be: someone who moves, someone who stays strong, someone who keeps showing up for his own health.

You're doing the same thing in your own way.

Maybe you take a short walk after dinner.

Maybe you check in on a friend every Sunday.

Maybe you read before bed instead of scrolling.

Maybe you cook at home more often than not.

Maybe you pause before reacting in a conversation.

These are not small things.

They are evidence of who you already are.

And once you see that, something shifts.

You stop thinking, "I need to become a more intentional person," and start realizing,

"I already am one — now I'm just refining it."

Why This Matters for Building New Habits

When you recognize the intentional habits you already have, you gain three advantages:

- You build from strength, not deficiency. You're not fixing yourself — you're expanding what's already working.
- You reinforce your identity. Your existing habits confirm that your Step Two identity wasn't wishful thinking. It was already emerging.
- You create a natural bridge to new habits. If you can walk the golf course, you can walk after dinner. If you can make coffee for your partner, you can build a gratitude habit. If you can read before bed, you can add five minutes of reflection.

Your past behavior becomes proof that you can build the future you want.

Choose One Habit That Reinforces Who You're Becoming

Now that you've uncovered the habits you're already practicing — the quiet, intentional actions that have been supporting you without fanfare — it's time to build on that momentum.

This is where Steps 1–3 come back into play.

You've already:

- identified the gap between where you are and where you want to be
- clarified the identity you're growing into
- set objectives that align with that identity

Now you get to choose one habit that reinforces all of that. Not five. Not ten. Just one.

A single, well-designed habit can shift the trajectory of your day, and your life, far more than a long list you'll abandon by next Tuesday.

Here's how to choose the right one.

1. Return to Your Identity Statement (Step Two)

Look back at the identity you wrote earlier — the person you're becoming.

Maybe it was:

- "I'm someone who moves every day."
- "I'm someone who stays connected to the people I love."

- "I'm someone who takes care of my health."
- "I'm someone who keeps learning."
- "I'm someone who shows up with patience and presence."

Your new habit should be a visible expression of that identity — something small enough to repeat, but meaningful enough to matter.

2. Connect It to One of Your Objectives (Step Three)

Your objectives gave you direction.

Your habit will give you traction.

Look at your objectives and ask:

What's one small action that would move me toward this?

If your objective is to improve your cardiovascular health, your habit might be a 10-minute walk after lunch.

If your objective is to strengthen your relationship, your habit might be sending one thoughtful message a day.

If your objective is to reduce stress, your habit might be two minutes of breathing before you open your laptop.

Keep it small. Keep it obvious. Keep it aligned.

3. Use Your Existing Habits as a Launchpad

This is where my 84-year-old friend's example becomes powerful. He didn't start from scratch. He simply extended a choice he was already making — walking — and it shaped his health for decades.

You can do the same.

Look at the habits you uncovered earlier and ask:

What's one natural next step?

If you already walk the dog, maybe you add a short stretch afterward.

If you already read at night, maybe you add a two-minute reflection.

If you already make coffee for your partner, maybe you add a moment of gratitude.

If you already take the stairs, maybe you add one extra flight.

You're not reinventing yourself.

You're extending what's already working.

4. Make It So Easy You Can't Not Do It

This is the part most people skip.

Your habit should be:

- small enough to do on your worst day
- obvious enough that you don't have to think about it
- rewarding enough that you feel good afterward

If it feels heavy, shrink it. If it feels complicated, simplify it. If it feels forced, choose something that fits your life better. A habit that's too big becomes a burden. A habit that's small becomes a rhythm.

5. Write It Down in One Sentence

Here's the format:

"Because I am someone who ________, I will ________ every day after I ________."

Examples:

- "Because I am someone who moves every day, I will walk for 10 minutes after lunch."
- "Because I am someone who stays connected, I will send one thoughtful message after breakfast."
- "Because I am someone who takes care of my health, I will drink a glass of water when I wake up."

This sentence is your bridge from identity to action.

How to Make Your Habit Stick (Without Forcing It)

Once you've chosen your new identity-based habit, the next step is making it part of your daily rhythm. Not through discipline. Not through guilt. Not through sheer determination.

Through design.

Habits don't stick because you try harder. They stick because you make them easier to start and more satisfying to complete.

Here's how to set yourself up for success.

1. Anchor Your Habit to Something You Already Do

The easiest way to start a new habit is to attach it to an existing one.

Your day is already full of anchors — moments that happen reliably, without effort.

Examples:

- After I pour my morning coffee, I take three slow breaths.
- After I walk the dog, I stretch for two minutes.
- After I brush my teeth, I read one page.
- After I close my laptop, I write down one win from the day.

Anchoring removes the hardest part of habit formation: remembering.

Your existing routine becomes the cue.

2. Prepare Your Environment to Support You

Your environment is always shaping your behavior — often more than motivation ever could.

Make your habit easier by adjusting your surroundings:

- Put your walking shoes by the door.
- Leave your journal on your pillow.
- Keep a water bottle on your desk.

- Place your vitamins next to your coffee mug.
- Put your book on the nightstand, not your phone.

When your environment nudges you in the right direction, the habit becomes the path of least resistance.

3. Shrink the Habit Until It Feels Effortless

If your habit feels heavy, shrink it.

If it feels complicated, simplify it.

If it feels intimidating, break it in half.

The goal is not to impress anyone.

The goal is to repeat it.

Examples of shrinking:

- 30-minute walk → 5-minute walk
- 10 pages of reading → 1 page
- 20-minute meditation → 2 minutes
- Daily journaling → one sentence

Small habits compound.

Big habits collapse.

4. Make It Emotionally Rewarding

A habit sticks when it feels good — not necessarily in a big way, but in a meaningful one.

You can create that feeling by:

- noticing how you feel afterward
- tracking your habit with a simple checkmark
- pairing it with something enjoyable
- acknowledging the identity it reinforces

This is the quiet satisfaction my 84-year-old friend feels when he walks the golf course. He doesn't celebrate it. He doesn't track it. He doesn't post about it. But he feels the benefit — and that's enough to keep him going.

Your habits should feel like that:

small wins that reinforce who you are becoming.

5. Don't Aim for Perfection — Aim for Continuity

You will miss days. Everyone does. Missing a day doesn't break a habit. Quitting does.

But here's the nuance that matters:

consistency can be a powerful ally — as long as it's gentle, not punishing.

When my kids were learning violin, I discovered something important. They didn't need perfect practice sessions. They didn't need long ones either. What helped them improve was simply showing up — even for a few minutes — because consistency created its own momentum. The act of returning to the instrument made the next day easier, and the next day after that.

Habits work the same way.

Consistency gives you a rhythm to fall back into.

It keeps the habit alive.

It keeps the identity warm.

But consistency should never become a weapon you use against yourself.

So here's the balance:

- Use consistency when it helps you. Let it be the gentle nudge that keeps your habit alive.
- Release perfection when it hurts you. A missed day is not a failure — it's just a pause.
- Don't let the miss become the new habit. Simply return to the rhythm the next time the cue appears.

The goal isn't an unbroken streak.

The goal is an unbroken identity.

6. Revisit Your Habit After Two Weeks

After two weeks, check in with yourself:

- Does this habit still align with my identity?
- Does it feel too big? Too small?
- Is there a natural next step?
- Is it supporting the objective I set in Step Three?

Habits are living things.

You're allowed to adjust them.

In fact, adjusting them is a sign of intention — not failure.

Step Four is where intention becomes visible.

You've uncovered the habits you already practice, chosen one new habit that reflects who you're becoming, and learned how to make it stick without relying on motivation or perfection. This is the quiet work that shapes a life — small actions, repeated with care, aligned with the identity you're growing into. You don't need dramatic routines or flawless streaks. You just need rhythms that support the person you've chosen to be. And now you have them. You've built the bridge between intention and action.

Now that you've created a habit that expresses your identity, it's time to zoom out. A single habit is powerful, but habits don't live in isolation — they live inside systems. Systems are the structures, routines, and environments that make your habits easier to repeat and your goals easier to reach. If habits are the daily expression of who you are, systems are the scaffolding that holds your life together. In Step Five, we'll build the systems that support your identity long-term, so your habits don't depend on willpower, mood, or circumstance. This is where your intentional life becomes sustainable.

Most people try to change their lives by focusing on individual actions. But actions are only as strong as the system they live in. A good system makes the right behaviors easier and the wrong ones harder. A weak system forces you to rely on willpower, motivation, or luck — and none of those are reliable long-term.

You've already done the hard work: you've clarified your identity, set meaningful objectives, and built habits that express who you're becoming. Now it's time to zoom out and design the environment that supports those habits day after day, season after season.

This isn't about creating a rigid schedule or a color-coded life. It's about building simple, supportive structures that make your intentional choices feel natural. Systems don't constrain you — they free you. They reduce friction, protect your energy, and give your habits a place to live.

In Step Five, we're going to build the systems that make your intentional life sustainable. Not perfect. Not optimized. Just supportive, steady, and aligned with the person you've chosen to be.

Step One — Conduct a Gap Analysis
Step Two — Formalize a New Self-Image
Step Three — Develop Clear Objectives
Step Four — Build the Habits That Bring Your Identity to Life
Step Five — Build the Systems That Support Your Life
Step Six — Bring It All Together

What a System Actually Is (and What It Isn't)

Before we start building your systems, we need to clear up a common misunderstanding. Most people hear the word system and immediately think of rigid schedules, complicated planners, or color-coded calendars. That's not what we're doing here.

A system is simply the structure that makes your habits easier to repeat and your life easier to live. It's the quiet architecture behind your days — the routines, environments, and defaults that support the person you're becoming.

Think of it this way:

- A habit is an action.
- A system is the environment that makes that action possible.

A habit is "I walk every morning."

A system is "My shoes are by the door, my mornings are uncluttered, and my dog expects the walk."

A habit is "I read before bed."

A system is "My phone stays in the kitchen, my book is on the nightstand, and my bedtime is consistent."

A habit is "I stay connected to the people I love."

A system is "I have a weekly check-in rhythm, reminders that support me, and a mindset that prioritizes relationships."

Systems are not about control. They're about support. They reduce friction. They protect your energy. They make the right choice the easy choice. And here's the part most people miss:

You already have systems — they just may not be intentional ones.

If your mornings feel rushed, that's a system.

If your evenings drift into screen time, that's a system.

If you always feel behind, that's a system too.

Systems don't care whether they help you or hurt you.

They simply run in the background, shaping your days.

Step Five is about bringing those systems into the light so you can design them intentionally — not perfectly, not rigidly, but in a way that supports the identity you chose back in Step Two.

This isn't about creating a life that looks organized on paper. It's about creating a life that feels aligned in practice. When your systems support you, your habits become easier, your objectives become achievable, and your identity becomes lived rather than imagined. That's the work we're stepping into now.

Why Systems Matter More Than Motivation

Most people blame themselves when they can't stick to a habit.

They assume they're lazy, undisciplined, or lacking willpower.

But the truth is far simpler — and far kinder:

It's not you. It's your system.

Motivation is unreliable.

It fluctuates with sleep, stress, mood, weather, hormones, workload, and a hundred other variables you can't control. If your habits depend on motivation, they'll collapse the moment life gets busy, messy, or unpredictable.

Systems, on the other hand, don't fluctuate.

They don't care whether you're tired or energized, stressed or calm, inspired or distracted.

A good system carries you even when your motivation disappears.

Think of it this way:

- Motivation is a spark.
- Systems are the wiring that keeps the lights on.

Motivation gets you started. Systems keep you going.

My 84-year-old friend doesn't walk the golf course because he wakes up every week feeling wildly motivated. He walks because his system supports it: he plays with the same group, at the same course, with the same rhythm, and walking has simply become the default. His system makes the healthy choice the easy choice.

That's the power of systems. They turn good intentions into reliable outcomes. Here's why systems matter more than motivation:

- Systems Reduce Friction. When your environment, routines, and defaults support your habits, you don't have to fight yourself. Your life becomes aligned instead of resistant.
- Systems Protect You from Low-Energy Days. You don't need to feel inspired to follow a system. You just follow the structure you've already designed.

- Systems Make Success Predictable. Motivation is emotional. Systems are mechanical. When you rely on systems, your progress becomes steady, not sporadic.
- Systems Free Up Mental Energy. A good system removes decision fatigue. You don't waste energy debating whether to do the habit — the system decides for you.
- Systems Create Identity Stability. When your systems support your identity, you don't have to constantly "try" to be the person you want to become. You simply live inside structures that reinforce that identity.

This is why Step Five is so important.

You've built habits that reflect who you're becoming — now you're building the systems that make those habits sustainable. Motivation may come and go. But a well-designed system keeps you aligned, steady, and moving forward.

The Three Types of Systems Every Intentional Life Needs

When people hear the word system, they often imagine something complicated — a detailed planner, a rigid schedule, or a set of rules that feels more like homework than support. But the most effective systems are simple. They're the quiet structures that make your life easier, your habits more reliable, and your identity more stable.

Every intentional life is supported by three types of systems:

1. Environmental Systems
2. Rhythm Systems
3. Accountability Systems

Each one plays a different role, and together they create the scaffolding that holds your habits — and your identity — in place.

Let's break them down.

1. Environmental Systems: Shape the Space, Shape the Behavior

Your environment is always influencing you — often more than motivation or willpower ever could. Environmental systems are the physical cues, layouts, and defaults that make the right behaviors easier and the wrong ones harder.

Examples:

- Keeping your walking shoes by the door
- Leaving your book on the nightstand
- Storing healthy food at eye level
- Keeping your phone out of the bedroom
- Setting up a workspace that reduces distraction

These systems don't require effort.

They simply nudge you in the direction you want to go.

When your environment supports your identity, your habits feel natural instead of forced.

2. Rhythm Systems: The Repeating Patterns That Carry You

Rhythm systems are the predictable patterns in your day or week that give your habits a place to live. They're not rigid schedules — they're gentle structures that create consistency without pressure.

Examples:

- A morning routine that anchors your day
- A weekly check-in with someone you care about
- A Sunday reset that prepares you for the week
- A nightly wind-down that signals rest
- A weekly movement rhythm (like my friend's golf walk)

Rhythms create stability. They reduce decision fatigue. They give your habits a natural home. When your rhythms align with your identity, your days feel coherent instead of chaotic.

3. Accountability Systems: The Structures That Keep You Connected

Accountability systems aren't about pressure or guilt. They're about connection — to yourself, to your goals, and sometimes to other people. These systems help you stay aligned when life gets busy or distracting.

Examples:

- A simple habit tracker
- A weekly reflection
- A partner you check in with
- A shared goal with a friend
- A monthly review of your objectives

Accountability systems don't judge you. They remind you. They help you notice when you're drifting and gently guide you back to center.

Why These Three Systems Matter

Each system supports a different part of your intentional life:

- Environmental systems reduce friction
- Rhythm systems create consistency
- Accountability systems maintain alignment

Together, they form a supportive structure that makes your habits sustainable and your identity lived rather than imagined. You don't need all three to be perfect. You just need them to be intentional.

In the next section, we'll start designing systems that fit your real life — not an idealized version of it, but the life you're actually living today.

How I Use These Systems in My Own Life

To make this practical, let me show you how these three types of systems show up in my world. None of them are fancy. None of them require apps or complicated planning. They're just small structures that make my habits easier and my days smoother.

These examples aren't meant to be copied. They're meant to show you how simple and personal systems can be.

1. My Environmental System: The Office That Runs My Life

My office is my hub. It's where almost every part of my day begins or ends. To be clear, "office" might be too formal a word—it's actually a shared space with our dining room. From my desk chair, I can see the front yard of the house, the living room, the family room, and the kitchen. When the kids were younger, it was noisy and chaotic, but even then, I loved working from here. It fits the way my life actually works: a hybrid of work and personal time from the moment I wake up until the moment I go to bed.

And while it may look like a collection of "stuff," that collection is my environmental system.

Here's what lives within arm's reach:

- Four pairs of shoes: walking, biking, gym, and casual slip-ons
- All my biking gear: helmet, gloves, heart-rate strap, bike computer, air pump, headset
- All the dog gear: leash, treats, bags
- My work equipment: PC, files, notebooks

Everything has a place (mostly).

Everything is visible.

Everything is ready.

I don't waste time hunting things down. I don't lose momentum switching activities. My environment supports the rhythms of my day—movement, work, connection, and care for Tessa. It's not minimalist. It's intentional.

And that's the point.

2. My Rhythm Systems: The Patterns That Carry Me

You've already seen my morning routine—Tessa, Ann's coffee, my Fitbit check, a quiet start. It's automatic now. And because it involves a German Shepherd, it's guaranteed. If you've ever lived with one, you know: they run the household schedule. My morning rhythm isn't just a routine; it's a partnership.

But I have other rhythms too.

One of my favorites is our Saturday night date night. It's simple, predictable, and grounding. It's a rhythm that supports connection with my wife, and because it's part of the weekly pattern, it doesn't get lost in the noise of life.

Rhythms like these don't require effort.

They create stability.

They give your habits a home.

3. My Accountability Systems: The Structures That Keep Me Aligned

I've shared how important the buddy system is for my workout consistency. My neighbor and I support each other, encourage each other, and—most importantly—expect each other to show up. We aim for at least two gym visits per week, and that shared commitment is incredibly effective.

Another accountability system is my Fitbit. It gives me clear, objective feedback on my movement, sleep, and recovery. It doesn't judge me. It simply reflects reality back to me. And that reflection helps me stay aligned with the identity I'm trying to live.

Accountability doesn't have to be heavy. It just has to be honest.

What These Systems Have in Common

None of these systems are complicated.

None of them require perfection.

None of them were built overnight.

They evolved because they support the life I want to live.

- My environment makes my habits easier.
- My rhythms make my days smoother.
- My accountability keeps me aligned.

That's all a system is: a structure that supports the identity you're choosing.

How You Can Begin Designing Your Own Systems

You don't need to build all three types at once. You don't need to overhaul your life. You don't need to create anything elaborate.

Start with the habit you designed in Step Four and ask one simple question:

"What small structure would make this easier?"

That's your first system. Maybe it's placing something where you'll see it. Maybe it's pairing the habit with an existing rhythm. Maybe it's asking someone to check in with you. Maybe it's preparing something the night before.

Keep it small.

Keep it supportive.

Keep it aligned with who you're becoming.

Systems aren't about control. They're about freedom. And that takes us to step six.

Step One — Conduct a Gap Analysis
Step Two — Formalize a New Self-Image
Step Three — Develop Clear Objectives
Step Four — Build the Habits That Bring Your Identity to Life
Step Five — Build the Systems That Support Your Life
Step Six — Bring It All Together

You've done the work. You've looked inward, clarified who you're becoming, set meaningful objectives, built habits that express your identity, and designed systems that support your life.

Step Six is simply about integration — taking all of that and weaving it into the fabric of your days.

This isn't another assignment.

It's an invitation.

Intentional living doesn't happen in a single moment. It happens in the small choices you make, the rhythms you follow, the systems you build, and the identity you reinforce day after day. You don't need to perfect any of this. You just need to live it — gently, consistently, and with awareness.

Here's what integration looks like:

- You notice when your actions align with your identity.
- You adjust when something feels off.
- You refine your systems as your life evolves.
- You celebrate the small wins that reinforce who you're becoming.
- You return to your habits when you drift — without judgment.

Integration is not about doing more. It's about being more of who you've chosen to be.

You now have a framework you can return to anytime your life feels out of alignment:

- Step One (awareness) reminds you to pause and notice.
- Step Two (identity) reconnects you with your identity.
- Step Three (objectives) gives you direction.
- Step Four (habits) gives you traction.
- Step Five (systems) gives you support.
- Step Six (integration) gives you continuity.

This is your intentional life — not perfect, not rigid, but grounded, evolving, and deeply yours.

Chapter 12 Summary: Building Your Intentional Life Through Systems

You can't build an intentional life on guesswork — you need clarity.

- Step One: Conduct a Gap Analysis to understand where you stand across the 11 laws.
- Use the "Your Turn" sections as diagnostic tools to identify patterns, strengths, blind spots, friction points, and opportunities.
- A personal SWOT analysis helps you see your life honestly and without judgment.
- Awareness is the foundation — a system can only be built on truth.

- Step Two: Formalize Your Identity by choosing who you are becoming, not who you've been.
- Identity is the compass for every decision, habit, and system that follows.
- Your identity should be simple, memorable, and actionable.
- Step Three: Set Clear Objectives that align with your identity.
- Objectives give your identity direction and your habits purpose.
- Keep them few, meaningful, and achievable — momentum matters more than volume.
- Step Four: Build Identity-Based Habits that express who you're becoming.
- Anchor habits to existing routines, shrink them until they feel effortless, and make them emotionally rewarding.
- Use consistency as a gentle nudge, not a weapon — return to the habit after a miss without judgment.
- Step Five: Build the Systems That Support Your Life.
- Systems are the structures that make your habits easier and your life smoother.
- You already have systems — this step helps you make them intentional.

- Environmental systems shape your space.
- Rhythm systems create predictable patterns.
- Accountability systems keep you aligned.
- My own systems — my office setup, morning rhythm, date nights, workout buddy, Fitbit — show how simple and personal systems can be.
- Step Six: Integrate Everything.
- Integration is not more work — it's living your identity through small, aligned choices.
- Adjust when needed, refine as you grow, and return to the framework whenever you drift.
- You now have a repeatable process for intentional living: awareness → identity → objectives → habits → systems → integration.

When your environment, rhythms, and accountability align with your identity, your habits don't require willpower — they simply happen.

Your Turn — Put Your System into Motion

- Revisit your Step One insights — your patterns, strengths, and blind spots.
- Re-anchor yourself in the identity you chose in Step Two.
- Confirm the objectives you set in Step Three.
- Choose the habit from Step Four that best expresses that identity.

- Ask: "What small structure would make this habit easier?" Build one system — environmental, rhythm, or accountability — to support it. Keep it simple, visible, and supportive. Let it settle before adding another.

Return to the six-step process anytime your life feels out of alignment.

The Law of Systems Is Simple: Design the structure that supports who you're becoming.

➤ IT'S NOT WHAT YOU KNOW, IT'S WHAT YOU DO. ➤

You've spent this chapter building the structure of an intentional life — awareness, identity, objectives, habits, and systems that support who you're becoming. You've done the work most people never do. You've created clarity, direction, and momentum. You've built a life that doesn't depend on motivation or luck, but on design.

And now you're ready for the final step.

Because all of this — every law, every reflection, every habit, every system — is leading you toward something bigger than productivity, health, or longevity.

It's leading you toward joy.

Joy is not the reward at the end of the journey.

Joy is the journey.

It's the feeling of living fully while you age slowly.

It's the quiet confidence that your days matter.

It's the sense of alignment that comes from living a life you chose on purpose.

Chapter 13 is where everything comes together.

It's where the laws stop being tools and start becoming a way of being.

It's where you learn to live lightly, gratefully, and fully — not someday, but now.

You've built the foundation.

You've built the habits.

You've built the systems.

Now it's time to build the life that sits on top of all of it —

a life anchored in joy.

CHAPTER 13 — THE LAW OF JOY

The law of joy is simple: you age well when you live fully.

I'll admit, this book started out on a bit of a downer with the story of my dad's downward spiral. And we're going to revisit that one more time — but I promise we'll end on a high note. That reminds me of a funny story from my early sporting clays days. Whenever our squad reached the last station, I'd say, "Let's end on a high note," and the whole group would break into a perfect E-note for a few seconds. If we had a new shooter with us, they never knew what to do. It was a small, silly ritual, but it always made us smile.

So yes — we'll end this chapter, and this book, on a high note too.

But first, back to the story.

I am now the very age my father was when his spiral began. He took early retirement at 62. Work had been his entire "why." He was twice divorced (three times if you count the fact that he and my mom married and divorced each other twice), and he lived alone. When he stopped showing up at the office, he lost the one structure that gave his life meaning. His world began to shrink, and it never expanded again.

My sister — five years older than I am — and I have talked about this many times. We both agree that retirement was the beginning of the end for him. Looking back now, with a clearer understanding of the difference between drifting and living intentionally, I suspect the decline started even earlier.

Could we have done more? Should we have? Maybe. But like the old Harry Chapin song "Cat's in the Cradle," we were busy with our own young families. When we called to invite him into our lives, he'd tell us how busy he was. We knew it wasn't true. But time marched on, and his life grew smaller and smaller.

Which brings me to my first point about joy.

Joy only happens in the present moment.

It doesn't live in the past — that's where rumination and regret live.

It doesn't live in the future — that's where anxiety and fear live.

My definition of depression is "living too much in the past."

My definition of anxiety is "living too much in the future."

There is no joy in either place.

I try not to live there.

I learn from the past, then move on.

I plan for the future, but not from fear.

And now, here I am at the same "crossroads age" where my father stepped off the path. So how is my life different from his?

For one, I choose to keep working — because I enjoy it. The first half of my career was spent inside companies where I learned to double down on my strengths instead of obsessing over my weaknesses. That approach prepared me for the second half of my career, where I became self-employed and could fully leverage the things I was good at — and enjoyed.

As my competence grew, so did my confidence. I became more efficient, which gave me more time for family, hobbies, and the other laws that make life rich. So why stop now? Work keeps me connected — to partners, customers, suppliers, and new problems to solve. Sure, it's a headache sometimes. And yes, one day I'll retire and join my friends. But unlike my father, I have friends to join.

You may have noticed I jumped straight to Law 2 — competence — and skipped Law 1 - Purpose. Let's fix that.

I've touched on purpose throughout this book, but I haven't pushed hard on you to define yours yet. That was intentional. Purpose can feel overwhelming. I wanted you to work through Chapter 12 first — to build clarity, identity, habits, and systems — before asking the biggest question of all.

Why are you here?

People who drift rarely answer that question.

People who live intentionally eventually do.

My purpose is simple: I want to be the best version of myself so I can support the people I love on their journeys.

That means being physically capable of helping my wife of 40 years with whatever life brings — I learned that when she broke her leg and needed help for nearly a year. It means being emotionally present when she fought her cancer battles. It means being available for our adult kids as they navigate early adulthood. It means being a good friend. And it means not becoming a burden for as long as I can help it.

My purpose is simple — and simple is good.

My purpose is the root of my joy.

Now let's look at how the rest of the laws feed that joy — and this time, we'll take them in order.

Law 3 — the Law of Fuel — absolutely feeds joy.

But I can already hear a few whispers from the back row:

"How can Cheerios, a smoothie, and the same dinner framework be joyful? Isn't that boring?"

I prefer to call it friction-free.

Low friction is simple — and as we've discussed, simple is good. I know exactly how my body responds to my consistent diet: for weight control, for performance, and for staying as migraine-free as possible. That alone makes me very happy.

But there's more to it.

Because our meals are consistent and repeatable, so is our grocery list. And now that we shop online and simply swing by to have the groceries loaded into the car, we save a ton of time — time we can use for things that actually bring us joy.

And here's the 30,000-foot view (I promised my wife I'd use that phrase once, and only once, in this book):

research shows that the fewer decisions you make in a day, the more willpower you have left for the decisions that matter.

Like whether to have that second slice of chocolate cake.

Trust me — you'll smile more when you step on the scale if you keep your daily decision count low. A consistent diet does exactly that. Little things really do add up.

Of course, I can hear another protest:

"But walking around the grocery store adds steps!"

Sure it does — but those are golden retriever steps. The kind my old dog Lucy used to take when she stopped to sniff every blade of grass. They're not bad, but they're not exactly training. If you trade that hour of ambling for a swim, a run, a bike ride, or a brisk walk, you'll get far more joy — and far more health — out of the deal. And online shopping helps you avoid impulse buys that don't add joy in the long run.

And then there's the big one:

"Isn't your diet full of ultra-processed foods?"

Yes — technically. Cheerios, Ensure, Clif Bars, Honey Stinger waffles — all UPFs. I was concerned too, so I dug into the research. And here's what I learned:

It depends on how UPFs are used.

If you're healthy, active, and using UPFs as functional fuel to support a high cardio load and recovery, they can actually provide a solid macro profile. But — and this is important — my diet would not be ideal for someone sedentary. In that case, UPFs could absolutely lead to weight gain.

And not all UPFs are "junk."

Take my beloved Cheerios. They're classified as UP2F because they're extruded and fortified — but they only have one gram of added sugar. Trust me, you can do a lot worse.

I'm glad I got that off my chest. I hope it helps you too.

So yes — I really like my fueling strategy. I love the fresh fruit we incorporate. I love how it keeps me going in the gym and on the bike. And I especially love sitting across from my beautiful wife each night for our consistent dinner framework, where we take stock of the day and our lives.

That is joy.

Law 4 — the Law of Movement — absolutely moves you toward joy.

"Find something you love."

That's the whole secret. Simple, understated, and spot-on.

As you know, my movement routine is a mix of morning dog walks, gym sessions, bike rides, and frequent post-dinner walks. I genuinely look forward to each of these — every single time. But it wasn't always that way. You might remember: I was a reluctant gym rat. I had no idea how much I'd enjoy it until I tried it.

And that's my best advice to you:

If you're struggling to find joyful movement, try things. Try lots of things. Try them with a buddy. Try them with your spouse. Keep experimenting until something sticks.

Not everything brings joy to everyone.

Take my next-door neighbor — the one who got me hooked on the gym. We lift together, but that's where our fitness overlap ends (other than the triathlon training period and the occasional bike ride). I prefer to get my cardio on the bike. He prefers to run. He still invites me on his runs, and I still decline.

I don't understand running.

It jars my brain.

It hurts my joints.

And I have never — not once — experienced the "runner's high."

I think it's a hoax.

I'll run ten minutes on the treadmill after lifting, but if you ask me to run five miles, you'll hear a lot of protesting. I can cover that same distance much faster on my bike with far less agony. Yet my neighbor loves running. And you might too.

That's the beauty of movement:

There are endless options. One of them will bring you joy.

And trust me on the buddy system. We've talked about it already, but it's worth repeating: having someone to share your movement with amplifies the joy. For me, I like a mix. I love our gym sessions, but I also love my solo bike rides and dog walks.

Maybe that's because I get to sing on those.

Something I would never inflict on another human being.

What I lack in lyrical recall and the ability to stay on key, I make up for in volume. But honestly — singing while moving just enhances the joy.

I have another neighbor who rides too. She's really into it — but most of her rides are group rides. Same sport, totally different experience. That's the point: movement is personal.

There is something out there that will bring you joy and support your ageless journey. You might just need to be diligent — and a little playful — in finding it.

Law 5: The Law of Restoration (Don't Sleep Through This One!)

It's not a big stretch to understand how excellent sleep creates the conditions for joy. We've all had that morning when we wake up after a great night's rest feeling ready to take on the world. But here's the thing: great sleep is like an outcome goal. You don't get it by wishing for it. You get it by building the processes and performance that lead to it — not just in sleep hygiene, but across your entire intentional life.

And this is a perfect moment to step back and talk about the synergistic nature of the 13 laws.

Earlier, I encouraged you not to try implementing everything at once. If you want to eat the elephant, one bite at a time is the way to go. A couple of changes at a time is great. But living intentionally across all the laws? That's when things get 10x better.

Sleep is where I've seen this most clearly.

I used to be the poster child for insomnia. Making sleep-hygiene changes helped — as we covered in Chapter 5 — but something bigger happened when I started living intentionally across the board.

What happens when you gain confidence from competence?

What happens when your actions match your identity — when you walk the walk and talk the talk?

What happens when your diet and movement are in balance?

Your mind and body calm down.

You stop fighting yourself.

You become ready for rest.

And when you start getting solid restoration — night after night — something wonderful happens: your performance improves, which drives an upward spiral.

Live better → sleep better.

Sleep better → live even better.

Repeat.

I'm living this now. Twenty years ago, my sleep was a wreck. Today, I climb into bed knowing that more often than not, I'll wake up ready to attack my day with purpose — aligned with my purpose. Is it perfect? No. I'm not perfect. I still have the occasional anxiety-fueled night.

But here's the difference: those nights are usually fueled by excitement, not fear. While writing this book, I'd sometimes wake up at 3:00 a.m. thinking about a chapter or an idea. And oddly enough, losing sleep over something I'm passionate about doesn't impair me the next day the way fear-based insomnia used to.

Now, one important caveat.

If you're dealing with a physical or mental health challenge, please get treatment. The 13 laws are not a replacement for appropriate medical or psychological care. My program assumes a baseline of physical and mental health. No judgment if you need to address something first.

And one last soapbox message:

Alcohol… wrecks… sleep.

End of soapbox.

I hope you find joy in restorative sleep. It's absolutely possible when you live your intentional life — your true life.

Law 6: The Law of Measurement — Joy in Numbers? Yes, It All Adds Up

I've already admitted to my geekiness and love of numbers, so you won't be surprised that I find joy in measurement. But here's the good news: you don't have to be a numbers person to appreciate what measurement gives you.

Think of your metrics as a simple feedback loop — a quick snapshot of how your intentional life is unfolding.

Been dialing in your diet for a few weeks?

The scale will tell you something.

Dropped alcohol, started exercising, cleaned up your fuel?

Your sleep score and HRV will reflect it.

These numbers aren't judgments. They're signals.

They tell you whether your actions are producing the results you intended.

Just make sure the numbers work for you, not the other way around.

Metrics are a moment in time.

Context is where the insight — and the joy — lives.

When you interpret your numbers with curiosity instead of anxiety, they become a source of encouragement, not pressure. They show you that your efforts matter. They show you that you're moving in the right direction. And that is joyful.

Law 7: The Law of Experimentation - Try, Test, Iterate — Until You Find the Joy

If measurement shows us the results, experimentation is what creates them.

A curious mind is a joyful mind.

Curiosity keeps us young.

Curiosity keeps us engaged.

Curiosity keeps us moving.

"What if I tried this?"

"What would happen if I didn't?"

Our oldest used to ask that at age two — "What would it do if it didn't?"

Children are pure joy.

There's nothing wrong with adopting a child's mind as we age.

Experimentation is simply the adult version of play.

Try something.

Test it.

Adjust.

Repeat.

Every experiment — successful or not — teaches you something about your body, your mind, your habits, and your life. And that learning is joyful.

Law 8: The Law of Mindset - Adopt an Attitude of Gratitude — Joy Will Follow

Like many things I've tried — joining a gym, meditation, even grounding — I wasn't a fan of the idea of keeping a gratitude journal. It felt forced. It didn't fit my friction-free philosophy. Honestly, it felt like one more thing I was supposed to do rather than something I wanted to do. So no, I don't keep a daily gratitude journal.

But I do keep a simple Word file on my computer — a running list of things I'm grateful for, with items added whenever something meaningful happens. No schedule. No pressure. No guilt.

After a few years, the list has 48 entries. Some are big. Some are tiny — like the hummingbird that hovered near me on the back deck one morning. On days when I need a nudge, I open the file and read all of the entries. And it works. Every time.

At the bottom of the list, I keep a small set of personal aspirations — a reminder of who I want to be:

1. Listen better before responding
2. Stay focused on being in service to others
3. Put only positive energy into the universe
4. Be patient
5. Focus on effort rather than reward
6. Stick to my agenda and avoid letting others undermine my path
7. Be honest

Reading this list gives me a double shot of joy — a reminder of what has made me happy and a reminder of who I am becoming.

Lately, I've been experimenting with a small addition: each night I mentally tick off three things that brought a smile to my face. No writing. No structure. Just a quiet moment of noticing. It's a friction-free way to end the day, and I'm curious to see where it leads.

Attitude is personal. Gratitude is personal. My gratitude practice brings me joy. I recommend you experiment with your own.

Law 9: The Law of Lifelong Learning - A Sharp Brain Is a Youthful, Joyful Brain

"Use it or lose it."

We've all heard the phrase, and it applies to both the body and the brain. They both need consistent exercise — and the only way to make that exercise stick is to find something joyful enough to become a frictionless habit.

For me, that means being a serial hobbyist.

I love having a beginner's mind again and again.

"Going back to school" isn't a metaphor — it's a lifestyle.

Reading is part of that lifestyle too. A lot of reading.

And not to brag, but I'm currently riding a two-night winning streak in our nightly Bananagrams game. (Ann may have a different interpretation of the word "winning streak," but I'm sticking with my version.)

All of these things bring a smile to my face. They give my days texture and meaning. They keep my brain sharp. They keep me young. They are, in a very real sense, joy.

The formula is simple: Find what you love and enjoy it.

But simple doesn't always mean easy. It's easy to fall into a rut.

So get out of the rut. Try something new. Let curiosity lead you.

With all the technology available today, learning something new each day requires only modest effort. A simple "I wonder why…" is enough to start the engine.

And yes — you can teach an old dog new tricks. Persistence and curiosity are the keys. Even if it means taking statistics again in your fifties, like I did.

If I can do it, anyone can.

Law 10: The Law of Connection - Relationships Amplify Our Joy

Sure, I love riding my bike solo several times a week. It's one of my true "happy places." But the real joy doesn't come only from the movement — it comes from the connections, big and small, that surround it.

First, there are the people on the greenways.

The simple smile.

The wave.

The quick "good morning."

On the surface, these moments seem trivial. But they're not. They remind us that we're part of something bigger — eight billion people all making our way through life, each with our own story, each doing the best we can. Those tiny exchanges stitch us together as human beings. They matter more than we think.

And then there are the deeper connections — sharing the details of my rides with Ann, with her cousins in Poland, with my expert-rider neighbor. These conversations bring joy too. They're reminders that we don't exist in isolation. We're wired for connection. We're meant to share our lives, our stories, our small victories, and our daily adventures.

By design, we need each other. And by our own design, we can choose to live intentionally by leaning into those connections.

As a self-professed introvert, I understand the need for alone time. I need it to recharge. But I also relish the time spent with others — the laughter, the shared experiences, the simple presence of another human being.

That's where amplified joy lives.

Law 11: The Law of Discernment -Joy In → Joy Out

We've all heard the phrase "garbage in, garbage out." But what if we flipped it? What if we became intentional gatekeepers of what we allow into our minds?

When you focus on uplifting things…

When you choose expert advice from trustworthy sources…

When you turn down the flow from the firehose…

You create the conditions for joy.

It sounds simple, but it takes intentional effort — especially in today's social-media-fueled world. The firehose is always on. The doomscroll is always available. The noise is always ready to drown out the signal.

But here's the truth:

Controlling what I allow into my brain has had a profound effect on my sense of peace and joy. And it can do the same for you. One easy way to start?

Swap an hour of scrolling for an hour of living.

Trade the firehose for something that fills you up:

- A walk
- A bike ride
- A lifting session
- A conversation
- A hobby
- A book
- Something that makes you feel alive

When you choose with intention, joy follows.

Joy in → joy out.

Law 12: The Law of Systems - The Rubber Hits the Road — and the Guardrails Keep Us Joyful

Systems are where the rubber meets the road. They're the structures that guide the intentional life we've chosen. When we put the right systems in place — systems that reflect our goals, habits, and identity — they quietly keep us moving down the path we designed for ourselves.

Our goals shape our habits.

Our habits shape our routines.

And our routines shape our days — the building blocks of a life.

When those pieces align, something wonderful happens:

we feel in control of our lives. Not in a rigid, white-knuckled way, but in a calm, confident, intentional way. And that sense of control is one of the purest forms of joy.

Systems don't eliminate life's challenges — they give us guardrails. They keep us from drifting. They reduce friction. They make the right choices easier and the wrong choices harder. They free up mental energy so we can focus on what matters.

When a plan comes together — when your habits, routines, and environment all support the life you want — it's a joyful thing to behold. And when that happens day after day, you're not just living intentionally… you're crafting a life well-lived.

Not one dominated by externally driven intensity. Not one built on willpower or luck. But one built on consistency, clarity, and intention.

Systems don't restrict joy. They protect it. They create the conditions where joy can show up again and again.

Final Culmination — The Law of Joy: Live Fully While You Age Slowly

Joy is not something we chase.

Joy is something we create through the way we live.

Every law in this book — from purpose, to confidence, to fuel, movement, restoration, measurement, experimentation, mindset, learning, connection, discernment, and systems — has been leading you here. Not to a perfect life, but to an intentional one. A life where your days feel like they belong to you. A life where you wake up with clarity, move through the world with purpose, and end each day with a quiet sense of alignment.

Joy is not loud.

Joy is not dramatic.

Joy is not something you wait for.

Joy is the feeling of living in harmony with who you are becoming.

It's the moment you realize you're no longer drifting.

It's the moment you feel the upward spiral begin.

It's the moment you notice that your life — your real life — feels good.

Joy is the reward for living intentionally. And it is available to you every single day.

Chapter Summary — The Law of Joy

- Joy is found in the present moment, not in rumination or fear.
- Joy emerges naturally when your life aligns with your purpose.
- Joy is amplified by movement, fuel, rest, and the systems that support you.
- Joy grows through curiosity, learning, and experimentation.
- Joy expands through connection — with yourself, with others, with the world.
- Joy is protected by discernment — choosing what you allow into your mind.

- Joy is sustained by structure — the systems that keep you on your path.
- Joy is not an emotion you wait for; it is a practice you cultivate.
- Joy is the natural outcome of living intentionally, consistently, and compassionately.

A Different Kind of "Your Turn"

Before you turn the page and step back into your life, I want to leave you with the intentions from the loving-kindness meditation — the same intentions I use myself. You can offer them to yourself first, then to the people you love, then to your community, your state, your country, and finally to all people everywhere.

Let these words settle into your heart:

> May you be happy.
>
> May you be healthy.
>
> May you be at ease.
>
> May you be safe.
>
> May you find joy in your heart,
>
> and may you know peace.

Now offer these same intentions to the people closest to you.

Then to your neighbors.

Then to your community.

Then to your country.

Then to the entire world.

This is how joy spreads — quietly, intentionally, one heart at a time.

And this is how I want to leave you:

with joy in your heart,

with peace in your mind,

and with the confidence that you can design a life that feels fully your own.

The law of joy is simple: you age well when you live fully.

➤ IT'S NOT WHAT YOU KNOW, IT'S WHAT YOU DO. ➤

FINAL WORD — YOUR TURN TO LIVE INTENTIONALLY

Before you close this book, I want to leave you with one final reminder.

Nothing in these pages came from superhuman talent or extraordinary genetics. I didn't start out with perfect habits, perfect health, or perfect clarity. I drifted for years. I made mistakes. I learned slowly. I struggled. I course-corrected. I tried again.

What changed my life wasn't brilliance or discipline.

It was intention.

And here's something equally important:

These 13 laws are not rigid. They're flexible.

They're meant to be shaped, adapted, and personalized. The way I live them today is not the way I lived them ten years ago — and it won't be the way I live them ten years from now. Life evolves. Circumstances shift. Priorities change. And your version of intentional living should evolve right along with you.

You don't need to follow my exact routines.

You don't need to copy my systems.

You don't need to live these laws the way I do.

You just need to live them in a way that fits your life — your purpose, your values, your season, your reality.

If I can do this, you can too.

You don't need to be special.

You don't need to be fearless.

You don't need to have it all figured out.

You just need to begin.

And then begin again tomorrow.

The life you want is not built by knowing.

It's built by doing.

And so I leave you with the same words that have guided me — the words that have shaped this book, my habits, my systems, and my joy:

➤ IT'S NOT WHAT YOU KNOW, IT'S WHAT YOU DO. ➤

Acknowledgements

An entire cast of characters is required for the many stages we perform on during our short lifetimes, and writing a book is certainly no exception. I could fill pages with the contributions that helped this book become reality.

But in order to avoid turning this into a TV award-show speech, I'll keep it short. That comes with the risk of sins of omission. No offense is intended if my net is cast too narrowly and I miss valued contributions.

First, I want to recognize my wife, Ann, and my adult children, Kris and Katie. Ann — along with my friend, neighbor, and biker extraordinaire Kamila Khan, as well as my primary care physician, Dr. Greg Gibbons — were the "leaders of the band" in encouraging me to write a book on reversing aging.

Ann, Kris, and Katie were instrumental in reading early versions of the manuscript and offering thoughtful editorial input that made the book better. And the cover design Ann created is phenomenal. Her creative process — and the sheer number of iterations — continues to amaze me.

Doug Parsons also read early versions of each chapter as they were developed. Doug may be the most familiar with my writing, having helped me immeasurably with proofing the earliest versions of my blog posts. I could not have launched the blog without him, and I'm grateful he agreed to read the first versions of this book.

Dave Maxfield, author of *Up Your HRV* and two other books, generously shared his experiences and insight into how to navigate the publishing process as well as some editorial suggestions. I was a little lost until receiving his guidance.

And finally, I want to recognize my workout buddy, Giacomo Campinoti. I would be a much weaker person — literally — without him. Our shared perspiration has been an inspiration.

To all the others who listened to me babble about the book's progress, thank you for your indulgence. These little moments meant a lot.

Sources & Inspirations (A–Z)

Arseneault, Paul Guérin — Research on red light therapy and mitochondrial function (Frontiers in Physiology).

Aurelius, Marcus — *Meditations* (c. 180).

Bartlett, Steven — The Diary of a CEO podcast (2017–present); *The Diary of a CEO: The 33 Laws of Business and Life (2023)*; conversations on identity, behavior, self mastery, and long-term personal growth.

Bassham, Lanny — *With Winning in Mind* (1988).

Baumeister, Roy F. et al. — Research on ego depletion and self-control (1998).

BDJ Open — "Regular dental visits and oral health outcomes" (2024).

Blair, Steven N. et al. — "Physical fitness and all cause mortality" (JAMA, 1989).

Brooks, Arthur C. — *From Strength to Strength* (2022).

Brooks, David — *The Second Mountain* (2019).

Cacioppo, John — Research on social connection and well-being.

Carnegie, Dale — How to Win Friends and Influence People (1936).

Chamorro-Premuzic, Tomas — *Confidence* (2013).

Chiu, H. Y. et al. — "Magnesium supplementation for migraines" (Nutrients, 2016).

Clear, James — *Atomic Habits* (2018).

COSMOS Trial — Randomized trial of cocoa extract and daily multivitamin supplementation (2022).

Csikszentmihalyi, Mihaly — *Flow: The Psychology of Optimal Experience* (1990).

Darrin Donnelly — Mindset-focused sports fiction series (2017–present).

Davidson, Richard J. et al. — "Meditation and brain function" (Psychosomatic Medicine, 2003).

Duhigg, Charles — *The Power of Habit* (2012).

Dweck, Carol — *Mindset* (2006).

Eisenson, Howard J. & Martin Binks — *The Duke Diet* (2007).

Fitzgerald, M. D. et al. — "Age-related decline in VO_2 max" (Journal of Applied Physiology, 1997).

Fletcher, Emily — *Stress Less, Accomplish More* (2019); Ziva Meditation teachings including "Perfection Is a Prison," "Compare and Despair," "Beginner's Mind," and foundational Ziva techniques integrating mindfulness, meditation, and manifesting.

Fredrickson, Barbara L. et al. — "Loving-kindness meditation and positive emotions" (2008).

Fredrickson, Barbara — Positivity (2009).

Gawdat, Mo — *Solve for Happy* (2017).

Gottman, John & Julie — Relationship research and books.

Hall, Kevin D. et al. — "Ultra-processed diets and calorie intake" (Cell Metabolism, 2019).

Haidt, Jonathan — *The Happiness Hypothesis* (2006).

Hill, Patrick L. & Turiano, Nicholas A. — *"Purpose in life and mortality"* (2014).

Holiday, Ryan — *The Obstacle Is the Way* (2014); *Stillness Is the Key* (2019); Stoic Virtue Series (*Courage Is Calling* (2021), *Discipline Is Destiny* (2022), *Right Thing, Right Now* (2024), *Wisdom Takes Work* (2025)); *The Daily Stoic* (2016); Daily Stoic email meditations.

Huberman, Andrew — Huberman Lab Podcast episodes on sleep, light, and vision.

Hyman, Mark — *Young Forever* (2023); Food Fix (2020).

Jones, Andrew M. — "Dietary nitrate and performance" (Sports Medicine, 2014).

Kodama, S. et al. — "Cardiorespiratory fitness and mortality risk" (JAMA, 2009).

Kross, Ethan — *Chatter* (2021).

Lancet Healthy Longevity — "Oral health and disease link" (2024).

Lee, I-Min et al. — "Physical inactivity and major diseases" (The Lancet, 2012).

Lieberman, Daniel — *Exercised* (2021).

Loftfield, Erikka et al. — Prospective study on daily multivitamin use and long-term health outcomes (2024).

Loving-Kindness (Metta) Meditation — Traditional Buddhist practice (public domain).

Lyon, Gabrielle — *Forever Strong* (2023).

Mandsager, Kyle et al. — "Cardiorespiratory fitness and long-term mortality" (JAMA Network Open, 2018).

Maxfield, Dave — *Up Your HRV* (2023).

MetLife Insurance — "Ideal Body Weight Tables" (1943).

Monteiro, Carlos A. et al. — NOVA food classification research (2018).

Nestor, James — *Breath* (2020).

Newport, Cal — *Digital Minimalism* (2019).

Panda, Satchin — Research on circadian rhythms and time-restricted eating.

Penedo, Frank J. & Dahn, Jason R. — "Exercise and well-being" (2005).

Ratey, John — *Spark* (2008).

Roehrs, Timothy & Roth, Thomas — "Alcohol and sleep" (2001).

Ryff, Carol D. — *"Psychological well-being"* (1989).

Shaffer, Fred & Ginsberg, Jason P. — "HRV metrics overview" (2017).

Shawn Stephenson — *Sleep Smarter* (2016).

Tai Lopez — "67 Steps" program (2014).

Tennyson, Will — Exercise and fitness videos (2019–present).

Thayer, Julian F. et al. — "HRV and health" (2012).

Thompson, C. et al. — "Dietary nitrate supplementation improves cycling performance in hypoxia" (Journal of Applied Physiology, 2014).

UCLA Health — Brain training and cognitive training resources.

Van Dongen, Hans P. A. et al. — "Sleep restriction and performance" (Sleep, 2003).

Van Dyke, Dick — *100 Rules for Living to 100: An Optimist's Guide to a Happy Life* (2025).

Vohs, Kathleen D. et al. — "Decision fatigue and self-control" (2008).

Walker, Matthew — *Why We Sleep* (2017).

Wisløff, Ulrik et al. — "High-intensity interval training improves VO_2 max" (Circulation, 2007).

About the Author

Mike Rouleau is a writer, small-business owner, and lifelong learner who has always been drawn to the question of what helps people perform at their best. That curiosity led him back to graduate school in his fifties to study psychology and mental skills — work that began in the world of sport but ultimately reshaped how he approaches health, aging, and intentional living.

In *Ageless by Design*, Mike shares the routines, experiments, and mindset shifts that helped him move from drifting to steering his own life. He lives in North Carolina with his wife, Ann, and their dog, Tessa. Readers can reach him or explore more of his writing at mikerouleaumentalskills.com.

www.ingramcontent.com/pod-product-compliance
Lightning Source LLC
LaVergne TN
LVHW010638110826
845149LV00014B/2875

9798995688907